First published in Great Britain in 2016 by A Way With Media Ltd, Shrewsbury, SY3 7LN

Copyright © Stephane Borie 2016

The right of Stéphane Borie to be identified as the author of this work has been asserted by him in accordance with the Copyright, Designs and Patents Act 1988

A CIP catalogue record for this book is available from the British Library.

ISBN 9781910469071

Photography, editor, publisher: Andy Richardson

Editorial artist and production: Paul Naylor

Printed and bound by 1010 Printing Group Ltd, China.

www.awaywithmedia.com

For Lexie, Roxanne and Fabien, who make it all worthwhile

FOREWORD

I feel touched and privileged to write this foreword to The Frenchman and the Farmer's Daughters.

Stéphane was a member of my team at The Waterside Inn and served with distinction for eight years.

This book is an inspiring tribute and timely record of the many modern classic dishes he can rightly call his own.

I remember his work clearly, with fondness and respect and I feel proud of his achievements that are so well deserved, not least recognition by Michelin with the award of a star for The Checkers.

Stéphane has blossomed since opening his own restaurant with his partner, Sarah, and her sister, Kathryn.

Underpinning this success are not only his great attributes as a chef, including consistency, organisation, tidiness and meticulous attention to detail but his warmth and personality.

When people first meet him, they see a strong guy with no hair but don't be mistaken, he is a real softie, a friendly guy!

Just today, I was looking at a few of his recipes and photographs and would love to sample some of his dishes for dinner or lunch.

His cuisine is exceptional and there are a number of stand-out recipes, like his assiette of suckling pig: that type of cooking is totally him.

Stéphane always had an impressive work ethic. He was the first to arrive every day, he was never late and he was always the last to leave. He had sheer dedication with a hunger to learn.

When it came to food, there was no compromise, nothing less than the best for Stéphane. That philosophy has stood him in good stead.

Young people who work for themselves must learn not to compromise because the client quickly detects cutting of corners. Stéphane knew that from the start.

CHECKERS
montgomery

When he joined us, although young, he quickly became one of the most important members of the brigade. And he maintained that level throughout his time with us.

But Stéphane wasn't the only stand-out person in my kitchen. I clearly and affectionately recall Sarah, who would become his partner.

This book and dishes within are certainly Stéphane's, but Sarah deserves much credit for helping him become a better version of himself.

Sarah taught him to think carefully before making decisions.

I gently perceived the early flickers of their budding romance and felt happy for them although it was imperceptible to the other chefs, since Stéphane and Sarah were consummate professionals. And like most successful couples, they complement each other well.

There were times when Stéphane could be a bit forceful, but Sarah calmed him down. Stéphane learned to turn his tongue seven times in his mouth

before he started to talk. Most importantly, Sarah is also an impressive talent in her own right, a real artist and one of the best pâtissieres I have known.

I think we all happened to need each other, fate kindly brought us together at The Waterside Inn.

I only regret not having known them better socially since I recall Stéphane's easy humour at our annual staff parties, they were always popular guests.

In many ways, Stéphane is what I would call a 'true chef'. There are chefs and then rarely, there are proper chefs, like Stéphane, he is one of the few.

Hundreds of people have passed through my kitchen during the past 45 years and he is among the top ten.

He was a young gem when he came to us and now he shines very brightly.

I salute Stéphane and wish him all the best with The Frenchman and the Farmer's Daughters.

He is a true chef.

Michel Roux, OBE
Global Ambassador
The Waterside Inn,
Three Michelin Stars

CHECKERS
montgomery

INTRODUCTION

When I first arrived at The Checkers, my only thought was to keep the business afloat during our first 12 months.

Kathryn, Sarah and I had made a go of things at our first restaurant, The Herbert Arms, though we were all keen to work in a venue that had greater refinement.

We found it here in beautiful Montgomery.

And since receiving the keys to our restaurant, we have worked tirelessly to make it a success.

Of course, our stories date back to a much earlier time. Sarah and Kathryn grew up on a farm and were surrounded by good food from an early age.

Sarah worked at The Waterside Inn, at Bray-on-Thames, which is where we met, while Kathryn had a very different career before moving into hospitality.

As a trio, we aim to ensure a warm and informal welcome and provide classic French fine dining and luxury accommodation.

As a boy, I did not imagine I would become a chef.

And yet I suppose it was somewhat inevitable.

I have a lot of happy memories of spending time with my family in rural France, where great vegetables and meat were at the table.

Cheffing also suited my temperament, I am a hard-working man who puts a lot of energy and effort into my work: those are the perfect ingredients for any cook.

Working at restaurants like La Tupina, in Bordeaux, and the three-Michelin-starred Waterside Inn were both instrumental in my development.

I learned about flavours and great produce, about finesse and refinement.

Both provided important lessons as I moved forward.

It was a great honour to have worked for some years under Michel Roux Senior and I am grateful to him for providing the foreword for my book.

Opening our own restaurant was the biggest challenge of my career.

Winning a Michelin star was one of the proudest moments. But I am also very proud of the way we go about our business.

We put the customers first, we constantly strive for improvement, we are determined to be the best.

The Frenchman and the Farmer's Daughters is a distillation of ideas and influences.

It tells some of our stories, it captures our origins, it explains how we arrived here. It also provides you with plenty of delightful recipes, some of which I hope you will try.

I hope you will enjoy reading The Frenchman and the Farmer's Daughters.

Creating my first book has been a labour of love.

I hope you will discover a little of what makes The Checkers so special. Merci et à bientôt.

Stéphane Borie,
August 2016

CHECKERS
montgomery

CONTENTS

CHECKERS
montgomery

DEVELOPING PASSION FOR FOOD

I fell in love with food as a young boy. Food was a bringer of joy, a source of contentment – it gave me something to look forward to.

I was born and raised in Agen, in south west France, near the river Garonne. We were 80 or so miles from Bordeaux. I was brought up by my mother, who worked as a cleaner, with my brother Joel and sister

Veronique, living in a tower block, Cité Rodrigues, in an unremarkable part of the city. We weren't wealthy, but she worked hard.

My mother was a fastidious, meticulous woman who strove to do her best. She didn't take a day off when she was sick – she didn't ask for sympathy, she just got on with it. They were aluable lessons to see as a

CHECKERS
stéphane's story

young boy, my mother passed on a great appetite for life and a determination to give of my best.

During holidays, I spent time with my grandfather, Marcel. He was a big influence on my life. He lived in Mussidan, a rural town that felt like it was a million miles from Agen.

I would go there during the summer holidays and enjoy every moment. My grandfather loved food and had his own potager, which is like an allotment.

It was located to the rear of his house and he would grow melons, courgettes and other fruit and vegetables. He took a great pride in his harvest each year. It was his pride and joy. He would also hunt, seeking out boar and rabbit with guns.

My grandfather would involve me with the potager, though he would never take me hunting. I was too wild, for a start. I think if he'd let me loose with a gun I might have shot at him rather than the rabbits.

He would fish too, and took me with him a few times. I distinctly remember the first time I got a catch. I took it off the hook and showed it my grandfather. "It is rubbish, it's a poisson-chat," he told me. "We can do better." He took the fish in his hand and threw it back in the river.

He kept chickens at home and occasionally he'd ask me to help catch them so that he could put them in the pot.

His chicken run had a door and he'd usher them towards it and position me so that I could catch one. Often, they'd bolt too quickly and I'd miss them. But I learned quickly and was soon an effective chicken-catcher.

He'd dispatch the birds and then we'd take them into a large shed, 'le cabanon' that was in his garden. I'd be charged with plucking them. It was a smelly, messy job and I didn't enjoy it. But I persevered.

My grandfather was a blunt and firm man but it is not just fondness and love that I remember him with – but gratitude.

Those lessons as a young boy have served me well – doing the rough jobs, showing endeavour and to only get praise when praise had been earned are all part and parcel of kitchen life.

CHECKERS
stéphane's story

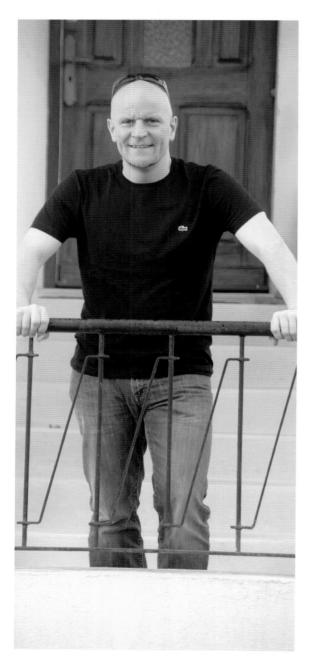

There have been numerous times when I've been in kitchens and I've caught a smell or flavour that reminds me of my grandfather.

I'm sure he instilled his love of food in me. Though he passed away when I was 12, his memory lives on and I love him to this day.

School was not really my thing, during those years I developed a love of football and heavy metal music, but I wasn't that interested in physics, history or geology. My passion was for food.

When I reached the age of 15-and-a-half and had my diploma "Brevet des colleges" it was time to leave school. I took an apprenticeship as a chef in Agen with Chef Jacques Porcell at La Malmaison.

Growing up in the kitchen was a good experience. Kitchens have a pack mentality where the younger, junior boys follow the leaders, or head chefs. You are all in it together, it's one for all and all for one.

I spent the first two years washing up but I enjoyed being part of a team and I was always hungry to succeed.

I obtained a diploma in 'Cooking Art' at the notorious (for the wrong reasons!) La Palme and eventually, I was offered a job at one of the most important restaurants in the Sud Ouest, La Tupina. A one of a kind, La Tupina is located in the historic district in Bordeaux, between Saint Michel and Sainte Croix.

It's pre-occupied with local produce and became a reference point for Sud Ouest traditions. I arrived for my interview right on time, but the owner, a charismatic man called Jean-Pierre Xiradakis, was an hour late.

I don't know whether he was impressed that I'd waited so long or whether he took pity on me. He asked me a few questions and then told me I could have the job.

He said he'd take me on, but if I didn't come up to scratch within a month I'd be out. Thankfully, I kept my job for a year.

CHECKERS
stéphane's story

La Tupina is evocative of a great countryside manor house, where the fireplace is at the heart of the home.

It has a large counter at the front of the house, which I recall was loaded with plump duck breasts.

There were cuts of perfectly-marbled, aged beef and beautiful pieces of pork. There were strawberries, loaves of bread, pieces of ham and more.

For me, it was an epicurean dream.

Dishes were assembled at the counter and then cooked over the fire.

Beef was seasoned and seared over an open flame while a wooden fire beside it was used to cook chickens on a spit.

There was a cauldron – La Tupina is the basque word for that – and in winter it would be used to heat soups.

During summer it would be replaced with a pan full of duck fat that would be used to cook golden, crunchy chips.

Little wonder it became an institution.

CHECKERS
stéphane's story

It is one of the most important establishments in the area and I learned an enormous amount by working there.

I'm sure that if people looked carefully at the origins of my food they would realise that I was heavily influenced by my time there.

La Tupina put brilliant produce at the heart of its menus and I have always done the same.

Good ingredients have always been king in my kitchen.

Of course, La Tupina has not been the only influence on my career. I've worked at a number of great restaurants and alongside many exceptional chefs.

There are things I've learned to do – and, more tellingly, learned not to do – from all of them.

At the age of 18, I was conscripted to the French Army for my National Service.

France no longer makes it compulsory for people to sign up, I imagine because it is too costly, though in my case I was thrilled to join.

I was based in Annecy, at the 27 Bataillion De Chasseurs Alpins, near to the Swiss border. I spent a happy and rewarding year skiing, hiking, building igloos and taking part in plenty of other outdoor pursuits. It was great fun.

For a sporty, heavy metal-loving, football-following 18-year-old, there was nothing not to enjoy. The army was a blast and I think more young men and women would benefit from the experience.

The one thing I didn't do during that year was cook. When my commanding officers asked me what talents I had, I decided not to tell them I'd worked as a chef. Chefs are revered in the army, particularly in France, because they feed the troops and keep people happy. But I wanted to ski.

> " I was based in Annecy, near to the Swiss border, and spent a happy and rewarding year skiing, hiking, building igloos and taking part in plenty of other outdoor pursuits. It was great fun. "

CHECKERS
stéphane's story

CHECKERS
stéphane's story

My family and friends imagined that I'd stay on. I'd been very enthusiastic about my time and they'd noted how much I'd enjoyed it.

But I always knew that it was a short-term thing. When my compulsory year came to an end I was ready to move on.

I had always known deep down that I would become a chef and it was time to seek another challenge. While I could have returned to La Tupina, I needed to find something new.

Any chef will tell you that he thrives on a challenge and I would have become stale if I had gone back to Bordeaux.

So instead, I decided to find my fortune in London. I got a job at L'Escargot, in Soho, and immersed myself in English culture while cooking traditional French food.

L'Escargot was in the heart of town, in Greek Street,

and has been an integral part of London's dining scene for almost a century. Its menu featured French classics, from lobster bisque to salade nicoise and from coq au vin to garlic snails.

It had welcomed the great and the good for generations. Princess Diana, Judy Dench, Coco Chanel, Mick Jagger, Elton John and Sir John Gielgud being among its patrons.

London provided me with an education. This impressionable boy from South West France learned quickly.

But I soon realised that city life wasn't for me.

Though London was vibrant and alive, I hankered for the softer rhythms of the countryside. I wanted to continue my culinary education in more bucolic surrounds.

Eventually, the fates conspired to provide me with the perfect opportunity.

CHECKERS
stéphane's story

I was invited for an interview at The Waterside Inn, at Bray-on-Thames, which was founded by Michel and Albert Roux.

Every chef will tell you that he wants to be the best – if not, then what is the point?

Those who say they are not interested in Michelin stars or cooking to the highest standard don't fool anybody – except for themselves.

I was thrilled at the prospect of working with one of Europe's greatest culinary institutions. After all, the restaurant had a remarkable pedigree.

When it was opened in 1972, it appointed Pierre Koffman as its head chef and he remained until 1977. In 2015, it became the first restaurant outside France to retain three Michelin stars for 30 years. It is truly remarkable.

I moved there with great expectation and wasn't let down. My first year was spent on the butchery section and the second was split between butchery and stocks and sauces.

I remain an avowed fan of The Waterside Inn. There are no restaurants in the UK that have enjoyed the sustained level of success that The Waterside has achieved.

And, speaking as a chef, I still marvel at the depth of flavour that is imparted in its dishes. The stocks and sauces are deeper, richer and more rewarding than those at any of its competitors. It is a remarkable restaurant and I felt very proud to work there.

Though Michel Roux Snr would work at the pass during my early years, the head chef was Mark Dodson. He is a good man and we remain close friends. Chef Mark spent 12 years at the pass and he was a great inspiration during my first three years. A calming influence and a man with great culinary skills, he was a remarkable mentor.

I learned more than I could imagine at The Waterside. The venue is sought out by young chefs and not all of them last the course. Few end up working on all of its sections.

I, however, was fortunate enough to do just that.

I started on butchery and particularly enjoyed the game season, when we'd receive hare, woodcock, teal and every other bird and beast imaginable.

I took time to learn how to make exceptional stocks and sauces and when my two years was complete I moved onto the vegetable and fish sections, spending a year on each.

Two years on the pastry section followed, which I thoroughly enjoyed. The Waterside has an exceptional reputation for 'patisserie' and I enjoyed the precision and attention to detail that comes with creating stellar desserts.

Moving around the different sections was a great experience. I would be asked to manage a section and the six chefs who worked on it, the equivalent of being thrown in at the deep end.

It usually took about three weeks to find my feet; dealing with the new dishes and pressures of managing a different team.

As my tour of the kitchen came to a conclusion after six hard-working years I was asked to go to work with Phillip Howard at The Square, in London.

I weighed up the pros and cons and confided in Michel Roux Snr. He was exceptional. He told me that he did not want to put me under pressure or in any way influence my decision.

He told me that if I thought it would be better for me to move on then I ought to. However, he also told me that I was viewed as management material and that I could look forward to a promotion if I stayed.

He was as good as his word and not long after I was appointed sous chef. And yet, paradoxically, I found that I had been happier working with the boys on one of the sections.

As sous chef, I found myself walking around the kitchen offering advice, checking seasonings and making sure standards were being kept at the highest level.

The thing I didn't do enough of was the thing I liked most: cooking. And so after two years, I decided it was time to move on.

I spent my last service running the pass, which was a great honour. Then it was time for a new challenge.

Le Manoir aux Quat Saisons, in Oxfordshire, had offered me a job as sous chef with a head chef position on the horizon.

I had also been approached to become the private chef for Lord and Lady Bamford.

The Bamford's offer was extremely attractive but I wasn't ready to step away from the kitchen and so chose to work for Raymond Blanc at Le Manoir.

Unfortunately, it wasn't for me. I underestimated what a solid knowledge and skill base The Waterside had given me – I soon realised the lessons I sought had for me, already been learnt, and I took up the position with Lord and Lady Bamford. Lady Bamford

famously founded the Daylesford Organic farm shops chain following the conversion of the family's farms in Staffordshire and Gloucestershire to organic.

I would cook breakfast, dinner and lunch on their 1,500-acre estate near Chipping Norton, in the Cotswolds, or cater for ladies' lunches, dinner parties, shoots and other functions.

I spent a year working for the Bamfords and parts of it were enormously enjoyable.

However, the lure of private work with high pay cheques, no budget menus and luxury travel was not enough.

I missed the kitchen environment, the pressure and the diversity. My journey was leading to an inevitable destination: my own restaurant.

CHECKERS
stéphane's story

CHECKERS
stéphane's story

CHECKERS
stéphane's story

During my time at The Waterside I had met my partner, Sarah. She'd been cooking there when I worked in butchery.

She is an exceptional chef, and her character suits kitchen life perfectly. She is as driven, competitive and as skilled as any man, and her kitchen humour is second to none. Her first words to me were criticism for the way I'd prepared a rack of lamb. We've never looked back.

Many years and three children later, we are the happiest of couples.

Sarah is a Shropshire girl and she and one of her sisters, Kathryn, wanted us to open our own restaurant.

Each of us invested an equal share and bought the lease on The Herbert Arms, in Chirbury. It was a traditional village pub about 20 miles from Shrewsbury, and was part of the historic Powis Estate.

It was a leap of faith. We had never worked as a trio before and there were no chefs of a similar calibre for miles and The Herbert Arms needed a lot of love.

But the rent was cheap, we had blind and unnerving faith in ourselves and we jumped in.

For a while, I wondered what on earth I was doing cooking at a pub in one of the UK's most rural counties.

There'd been a time when I'd been the private chef for billionaires.

I'd spent many years successfully cooking at Britain's most successful restaurant.

What was I was doing cooking at a pub in one of the UK's most rural counties?

I'd gone from three Michelin-stars to a venue where there was a pool table and darts board, not to mention karaoke on Saturdays.

But the restaurant gained good reviews and became very popular. In hindsight it was quite remarkable how quickly we became established — in those early days we had nerves of steel.

It was one of the most important stepping stones of my career.

CHECKERS
stéphane's story

CHECKERS
stéphane's story

After eight months, we heard about another venue, The Checkers, at Montgomery, just over the Welsh border.

We absolutely fell in love with the location and could see the potential in the freehold – a beautiful 17th century coaching inn crying out for a new lease of life.

We took the plunge and our offer was accepted.

CHECKERS
stéphane's story

It was mid-2009 and the country was on the cusp of economic meltdown. Securing the freehold funding was complex and time consuming, not least because we had only been in business a few short months. Our bank business manager Stephen Humphries' faith in us was absolutely key, without his backing and support we would not be at The Checkers now. This, together with the patience from John Whittingham, a local businessman who dealt with the sale, made the impossible possible, and the sale completed in November 2009. This was good old fashioned business.

The Checkers was overhauled top to bottom and we opened in March 2011. Things got going well — we had an existing customer base from The Herbert Arms and there was a real buzz about the town. The chaotic days of a new business saw us learning on our feet and our goal each week was to keep the balls in the air and just keep going.

To our astonishment within seven months we'd won a Michelin star. It was beyond our wildest dreams. Suddenly we were being feted by critics and visited by people from around the UK. We later found that Mark Dodson had been partly responsible for our success. He had tipped off the Michelin inspectors and suggested they pay a visit to us. They had visited anonymously — and liked what they'd seen and tasted. We celebrated by giving our guests a glass of champagne after dinner. It was a most memorable Thursday.

Since then, we've developed the restaurant by adding new rooms and in 2016 we refined the menu, offering a six-course tasting menu. The restaurant has never been so busy. We offer friendly service and an informal setting and we are sold out night after night.

The Checkers offers dishes that are rooted in tradition; they showcase my influences, from La Tupina to The Waterside Inn, and they have a strong French influence.

Food is presented in a modern style and we are proud to have retained our Michelin star for so long. Having refurbished our restaurant and rooms it is time for us to share some of our recipes with you They are our new modern classics and we hope you enjoy them.

Thank you for your support. Bon appétit.

Stéphane

- As a commercial kitchen we have specialist pieces of kit available to us.

Some recipes specify the equipment used as this is simply what we use, it is possible to do the vast majority of these recipes with domestic appliances.

Rational oven — In 2015 we were finally able to buy a Rational Oven. I had wanted one since our very early days but had to be patient!

This oven is an exceptional piece of kit and I would not be without it now. However, a combi steam oven would be a good alternative.

If you have a conventional oven and steam is required place a tray of water in the bottom of the oven.

Xtreme blender — this commercial blender is robust, is used many times a day and allows us to prep the vast quantities required.

A domestic jug blender would work fine too.

Hand blender — the hand blender we use is simply a commercial version of a regular stick blender.

Kenwood mixer — this machine is a fantastic addition to a home kitchen, particularly with all of the attachments, certainly one to be recommended. However, a regular mixer would be fine in the majority of recipes.

Dehydrator — this is a really useful piece of kit in a commercial kitchen. However, an oven on its lowest setting would work.

The water bath (thermocirculator) — this could be replaced by a large pan of water with a digital probe thermometer.

Knives — my preferred choice of kitchen knife is Wüsthof. These are fabulous knives.

Every Christmas we give our chefs a new Wüsthof knife engraved with their name.

Specialist produce — there are some specialised produce used in the recipes such as methylcellulose and agar agar. All are available on amazon.

CHECKERS
farmer's daughters

Trefonen is a beautiful village and New Barns Farm stands at the top, with stunning views of the Shropshire plains.

Our grandparents lived next door and family life and farm life were well and truly intertwined. Dad inherited the farm when he was 21 from his grandfather and he worked doggedly to grow it and have a successful business.

Lucky for him, when he met our mum, a headmaster's daughter from the Lake District, he met someone who had always wanted to be a farmer's wife. Mum and Dad epitomised team work and loved what they did.

With five kids and a growing business life was busy. In 1983 they started to process the milk and sell it door to door. We were surrounded by the business and everything else that came with it – customers, staff, banks and endless hassle!

As kids, being a farmer's daughter didn't always feel great or glamorous – but looking back it was difficult to beat. Winter meant snow, school closed and hours sledging in the barn field, walks through gigantic snow drifts and snow ball fights with dad.

Spring meant lambing time, two weeks with our cousins, pet lambs, frosty mornings, eggy bread and rosy cheeks. Summer meant silaging, sheep shearing and feeding the hungry contractors. As for Autumn, that was a time for bobble hats and crispy walks in the Candy Woods. All a bit feral and chaotic, but we loved it.

Mum and Dad were driven but the world of Michelin stars couldn't have been further from theirs – Stéphane laughs that Mum's signature dish is 'cheese on a plate'! But, from the very beginning they had faith in us and a childhood immersed in the reality of life and business has been priceless.

Their attitude has been 'go for it', and their absence of doubt has meant that we have always believed that we can do it.

Our Dad lives and breathes farming in a very similar way to the way Stéphane lives and breathes cooking. When you have grown up with this dedication and passion, understanding it is second nature.

New Barns is a special place and our childhood has informed all we do. The floor boards and bar top are from a huge sweet chestnut tree, which fell in a summer storm on the farm in 2006. Our favourite table in the restaurant was made by our maternal grandfather, Gramps, when mum lived in Ghana as a little girl.

Our parents, our childhood and New Barns is a big part of the success of The Frenchman and the Farmer's Daughters and you will see glimpses throughout The Checkers.

Kathryn Francis

CHECKERS
bordelaise food

PERFECT PRODUCE

My first job as a professional chef was in Bordeaux. As a just-left-school-apprentice, I started at the bottom, washing pots and pans.

I sweated in kitchens for two long, hard years and by watching the other guys in the kitchen I learned how to be a chef.

I absorbed their traditions, customs and behaviours; they became the foundations upon which I built.

Though I was born in Agen, Bordeaux somehow feels like home.

It has stunning architecture, a beautiful temperate climate and gorgeous public spaces, including verdant parks and the River Garonne.

I lived in an apartment in the centre of Bordeaux while I was working in the city and I have the happiest memories whenever I return.

My home now is in Montgomery, at The Checkers. Bordeaux remains a home-from-home and that's no surprise, for it offers exceptional cuisine. It is a chef's paradise.

The city's market, Marche des Capucins, was an exceptional source of produce when I worked here.

The freshest herbs, the best fruit and vegetables, the most tender meat, the best fish and stunning cheeses were all delivered to our kitchen door.

And if ever we ran out of supplies, we would be able to make a quick trip to the market to top up.

33

CHECKERS
bordelaise food

To this day, the market remains a first class location for brilliant, flavoursome, seasonal ingredients.

And the stallholders are all so knowledgeable. They are happy to talk about cheeses made from unpasteurised cow's milk or to recommend deliciously sharp gariguette strawberries that arrive early in spring.

They will recommend tantalising still-alive snails or talk with great authority about meat that is marbled with streaks of fat and has been dry-aged to maximise its flavour.

The city provides a wide selection of restaurants, including those that are Michelin-starred and those that are not, like La Tupina. Eating out is a heady experience. There is an endless choice.

The region is carnivore country and not just because of the exceptional cuts of beef that are available in plentiful supply. It provides a stunning catch of fish from the Atlantic, not to mention plenty of shellfish.

There are plenty of great fish restaurants that offer stunning fruits de mer. And one of the true joys of eating in such restaurants is that the ingredients come first: chefs don't need to do anything fancy to such brilliant ingredients.

Crab, langoustine, brown shrimp and other crustacean are cleaned, cooked and served — just the way nature intended.

The chefs respect them and let the natural flavours come to the fore.

CHECKERS
bordelaise food

It's not just sumptuous food that makes Bordeaux a gastronome's paradise.

It has some of the best vineyards in the world, particularly those surrounding St Emilion.

Places like Aux Quatre Coins du Voin have tasting machines that allow people to sample from a selection of 32 vintages.

It means people can taste grand crus at a reasonable price.

And there are many grand crus to taste.

St Emilion is one of Bordeaux's largest winemaking appellations and produces more wine than Listrac, Moulis, St Estephe, Paulliac, St Julien and Margaux combined.

The region's finest vineyards are found atop the steep limestone slopes of the village itself while a band of garagiste producers are eschewing terroir to make small-batch, deeply-concentrated wines from their homes.

My cooking is rooted in the traditions of South West France, where the produce is exceptional and good ingredients are respected.

It makes for some of the best eating in the world.

CHECKERS
montgomery

CHECKERS
recipes

CHECKERS
recipes

CHECKERS bread

CHECKERS SOURDOUGH BREAD & PAIN BRIOCHE AUX NOIX

> To make the sour dough starter:
>
> Combine 300g light rye flour with 350g water at 20c and leave for four days covered and at room temperature.
>
> The time lapse is important as this allows for the process of yeast development.
>
> The sourdough starter is the most important thing for our pain brioche aux noix and rosemary sourdough.
>
> It requires precise daily care and will ultimately define the quality of your bread.
>
> We feed the dough at the same time daily with: 75g light rye flour, and 87.5g water, which must be at 25c.
>
> A well looked-after and well-fed sourdough starter can live forever.

Ingredients – rosemary sour dough

500g	white flour
15g	salt
335g	water at 25c
210g	sourdough starter
2	chopped up rosemary sprigs, leaves only

Method

Put all the ingredients in a Kenwood mixer and knead for 5 minutes with the dough hook until homogenous. Squeeze some olive oil at the bottom of a round stainless steel bowl and place the dough inside.

Place a damp cloth on the top and leave in a warm place in the kitchen to prove for 90 minutes.

Tip the proved dough on the table and pull the 4 corners towards the centre of the dough (1st round). Repeat this operation once more (2nd round). Form the dough into a ball and return to the stainless steel bowl. Cover with a damp cloth and prove in the same spot as earlier for 120 minutes.

When sufficiently proved, repeat the operation and give it a 3rd and 4th round as before, adding the chopped rosemary in the centre before the 4th round. Place it in a cane bread basket for its final proving.

Put it back in a warm spot, cover with a damp cloth and leave it to prove for another 2 hours.

Pre-heat your oven to 225c (dry heat and full fan).

Place a pastry tray inside.

When ready to cook, tip the bread on the scorching tray and criss cross the top with a small sharpe knife.

Cook at 225c for 40-45 minutes.

Ingredients – pain brioche aux noix

500g	strong white flour
100g	sourdough starter
225g	water (20 c)
10g	fresh yeast
12g	salt
30g	caster sugar
80g	soft diced salted butter
175g	walnut halves

Method

In a Kenwood mixing bowl, add all the ingredients except the butter and walnuts.

Knead with the dough hook for 5 minutes at a low speed and 5 minutes at a high speed.

Add the butter until completely absorbed, like a brioche.

Then add the walnuts and mix a little more.

Cover the dough with a damp cloth and leave to prove in a warm area of the kitchen for 45 minutes.

Deflate the dough and prove for another 45 minutes.

When it has doubled in size, tip the dough on your working station and divide it into 5 equal portions.

Roll into balls. Leave to prove for another 15 minutes each.

Form the dough into a long loaf shape and slash with a sharp knife.

Cover the breads with a damp cloth again and leave to prove again for 90 minutes.

Egg wash and bake at 225c for 10 minutes and decrease the heat to 215c for 5 more minutes.

Take them out of the oven and leave to cool completely on a wire rack.

CHECKERS SOURDOUGH BREAD
& PAIN BRIOCHE AUX NOIX continued

BREAKFAST SELECTION

Yield — 6-8 portions

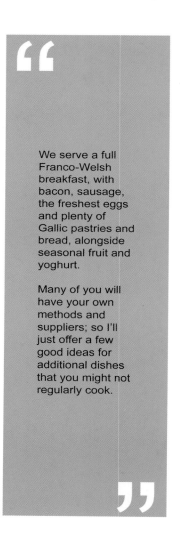

We serve a full Franco-Welsh breakfast, with bacon, sausage, the freshest eggs and plenty of Gallic pastries and bread, alongside seasonal fruit and yoghurt.

Many of you will have your own methods and suppliers; so I'll just offer a few good ideas for additional dishes that you might not regularly cook.

Marinated figs

This excellent recipe was given to me by Alice Bamford and is one of our guest's favourite morning fruits.

It's very easy to make and goes great with Greek yoghurt.

Ingredients

500g	water
175g	honey
2	cardamom pods
1	zest of a lemon (use potato peeler)
1tbs	grain mustard
15g	peeled and thinly sliced ginger
480g	dried figs

Method

Bring all the ingredients except the figs to the boil.

When boiling, add the figs and simmer for 2 minutes.

Transfer to a Le Parfait jar and leave to marinate for 24 hours before serving.

BREAKFAST SELECTION continued

Kouglofs

At The Checkers we offer these delicious, brioche-like treats from the Alsace region.

They are a bit time consuming to make but they are well worth the effort.

Equipment

Kenwood mixing bowl, with the dough hook
Specialist kouglof moulds (or dariole moulds)

Ingredients - Raisin syrup

125g	water
50g	sugar
125g	sultanas

Method

Bring the sugar and water to the boil, add the sultanas and take off the heat.

Leave to cool in the syrup.

Transfer to an air tight container and keep in the fridge. Macerate for at least 24 hours.

Ingredients – dough

220g	soft butter (beurre pomade)
45g	sugar
15g	yeast
75g	warm milk
10g	salt
315g	flour
4	eggs

Method

In a stainless steel bowl, whisk up the beurre pomade and the sugar until light and fluffy. Keep aside.

In a Kenwood mixing bowl, dissolve the yeast in the warm milk and add salt, flour and eggs. Knead with the dough hook for 15 minutes at speed 3. Increase the speed to 8 for 2 minutes. Lower the speed back to 3 then gradually add the butter/sugar mix until it is completely combined. Mix for 5 more minutes and increase the speed to 8 for 2 more minutes. Add the drained, soaked raisins and mix for 1 more minute.

Transfer the dough to a long plastic tray and cover with a clean kitchen towel until it has doubled in size, which will take about an hour. Knock back the dough and store in the fridge for 12 hours.

Divide into 100g balls.

Butter the moulds twice and place some peeled almonds in the base (or dents if using specialist moulds). Press the dough into each mould and prove in a pastry oven at 35c with 3% humidity for 1-2 hours. When plump and ready, cook at 180c for 10-12 minutes.

Turn out onto a pastry wire rack. Dust with icing sugar. Serve warm.

MARMALADE AU GRAND MARNIER

Homemade marmalade is a bit special – especially one finished with Grand Marnier.

January and February are the best times to make marmalade using Seville oranges

It is best to make it in small batches, which are easier to control. The quality is far superior.

Ingredients

1kg	Seville orange
100g	passed lemon juice
2.5l	water
2kg	granulated sugar
150ml	Grand Marnier

Method

Lay the sugar on an oven tray and warm it up in the oven at 65c.

While it's warming, put 3 ceramic plates in the fridge. Peel all of the Seville oranges.

With a sharp chopping knife, neatly julienne all of the skin and place it in a jam pan alongside the water and the lemon juice.

Cut the oranges in 2 and squeeze the juice out.

Pass it through a muslin cloth. Add the juice to the other ingredients in the jam pan.

Place the orange skin and pips in the muslin and close it with a piece of string.

Submerge it in the water with the lemon, orange juice and julienned orange skin.

Bring to the boil and simmer until it is reduced by half, which should take about 2 hours.

Remove the muslin cloth with a pair of tongs and squeeze out all of the juice.

Discard the muslin.

On a very low heat, add the warm sugar. Whisk it thoroughly until it has dissolved.

When clear, boil for 15 minutes, whisking from time to time. Add a small knob of fresh butter, which will help to separate out any impurities.

As the texture changes to become more marmalade-like, spoon a little of the mixture onto a one of your chilled plates.

It should set and wrinkle when pushed with your finger. If it does not, cook the mixture for a further 5 minutes and retest.

Remove from the heat and let the marmalade stand for 5 minutes.

Add the Grand Marnier and let it stand again for 30 minutes.

With a wooden spoon, stir again to spread the peel evenly.

Store in a sterilised Le Parfait jar.

Delicious with toasted and buttered brioche slices.

PRAWN COCKTAIL CRACKERS

> This funky take on a classic dish is always a talking point.
>
> It's not so difficult to make that you can't make it at home for your next dinner party.
>
> The crackers might look daunting but, with the exception of using an air gas canister, everything is reasonably straight-forward.
>
> A regular marie rose sauce would still be delicious – the canister just aerates the sauce.

Equipment

Tall blender
Combi oven
Dehydrator (or very low oven)
Deep fat fryer
Gas canister and 2 nitrous oxide cartridges

Ingredients

140g	tapioca flour
140g	cooked and peeled frozen prawns
1.25g	monosodium glutamate (msg)
2.5g	salt
	water, to achieve the desired consistency.

Method

In a tall blender, puree the prawns with msg and salt. Pass through a fine meshed tamis and transfer into a stainless steel bowl.

Mix the prawn puree with the flour using a little water, so that the mixture becomes homogenous and sticky.

Roll the mixture in double cling film into a sausage shape of 3cm diameter. Steam in a combi oven at 100c for 45 minutes, turning half way through. Reserve flat in the fridge and leave to rest for 48 hours.

On the day of serving, slice the roll at about 2mm and dry in the dehydrator (or very low oven) at 60c for 1 hour.

Deep fry at 180c. The crackers will instantly puff up. Remove immediately and reserve on absorbing paper towel, to drain off any excess fat.

Professional touch

**Marie Rose Mix
(to fill a gas bottle canister)**

Ingredients

300g	Marie Rose sauce
200g	double cream
50ml	milk
	fine salt, ground white pepper and cayenne

Method

With a marise, in a stainless steel bowl gently fold all of the ingredients.

Check the seasoning and adjust as needed.

Using a funnel, fill up the gas canister with 430g of the mix and load with 2 cartridges.

MARIE ROSE SAUCE

Ingredients

300g	mayonnaise
100g	tomato ketchup
6g	Worcester sauce
20g	cognac
2g	tabasco
	fine salt, ground white pepper and cayenne to taste

Method

In a stainless steel bowl, whisk all the ingredients together.

To assemble

Cut some prawn tails into 3 and season them with vinaigrette and place them on the crackers.

Shake the canister and squirt some Marie Rose foam onto the prawns. Dust with paprika and serve at once.

CHECKERS
canapé

BEETROOT MERINGUES AND HORSERADISH CREAM

"

Theses tiny, melt-in-the-mouth meringues were an instant hit when we introduced them at The Checkers.

They are intensely flavoured and became so popular that our canapé chef spent most of his time making them.

At one stage, we banned him from making any more and suggested keeping them off the menu. But our regular customers kept asking for them and we cracked under pressure.

They're one item that people can't get enough of. Even converting some guests who are not beetroot lovers!

This recipe yields about 2 medium trays of them.

"

Equipment

1 Excalibur dehydrator and trays (or very low oven)
Major Kenwood mixer with whisk and bowl
Baking parchment
Piping bag
Large plain piping nozzle
Soft plastic spatula

Ingredients

300g	raw beetroot juice reduced to 150g
15g	sugar
25g	balsamic vinegar
3.5g	methylcellulose F50
1g	Xanthan gum

Method

Boil the sugar and balsamic vinegar until the sugar has dissolved to make your gastrique. Allow to cool.

Into a tall jug pour the cold beetroot juice, the cooled gastrique, methylcellulose F50 and the xanthan gum.

Transfer this beetroot mix into a Kenwood Major bowl, with the whisk attachment connected. Whisk at full speed for at least 5 minutes.

It has to be light and airy. If the mix remains thick and does not achieve that consistency add a little water.

When the mix is homogenous transfer it to a disposable piping bag with a large stainless steel nozzle.

Pipe onto baking parchment and dry in a dehydrator @ 60c or a domestic oven for between 6 to 8 hours.

HORSERADISH CREAM

Ingredients

80ml	double cream
1	spoonful of Dijon mustard
3	spoonful of Coleman's horseradish cream
½	lemon juice
	table salt, ground white pepper and cayenne pepper

Method

Gently fold all the ingredients together until you get a consistency resembling Crème Chantilly.

Transfer to a disposable piping bag with a medium stainless steel nozzle and reserve in the fridge.

To assemble

Stick the meringues together with the horseradish cream and serve at once.

CHECKERS
canapé

PORK CRACKLING WITH ROASTED GARLIC MAYONNAISE

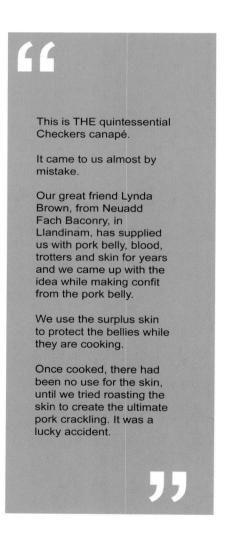

> This is THE quintessential Checkers canapé.
>
> It came to us almost by mistake.
>
> Our great friend Lynda Brown, from Neuadd Fach Baconry, in Llandinam, has supplied us with pork belly, blood, trotters and skin for years and we came up with the idea while making confit from the pork belly.
>
> We use the surplus skin to protect the bellies while they are cooking.
>
> Once cooked, there had been no use for the skin, until we tried roasting the skin to create the ultimate pork crackling. It was a lucky accident.

Ingredients

Cured Neuadd Fach Baconry pork skin, with a good covering of fat
Goose fat

Method

In goose fat, confit the skins for 10 hours at 98c, until well, well cooked. We cook the pork bellies with the skin although it is not necessary to do this. The skin should literally be falling apart.

Leave everything to cool in the fat, which should be overnight.

The next day, when cool and easier to handle, lay the skins on a cling-filmed tray with cling film between each of them.

Leave in the fridge for an additional 12 hours.

Now, partially score the skin every 1mm, which helps to make them even crisper.

Cut them as sticks, squares, triangles or your desired shape and keep them in the freezer.

When required, heat your oven to 230c and cook the pork sticks between 2 sheets of baking parchment sandwiched between 2 heavy trays for about 10-12 minutes. This keeps them flat and prevents them curling.

Now remove the top tray and top parchment for a further 5 minutes of cooking, which gives the skins a bubbly effect. Transfer the sticks onto a wire rack immediately.

Serve stacked in little pots with some roasted garlic or whole grain mustard mayonnaise.

CHECKERS
canapé

POTATUBES

Equipment

1 fryer (or a pan of oil and a hand held digital thermometer)
1 Chinese spiralizer
12 metal tubes
1 roll of baking parchment

Ingredients

3   large Maris piper potatoes
       salt

Method

First, set the fryer at 100c. Then, using the spiralizer, create long spaghetti of potato.

Dip the potato in the fryer and pre-cook it for 5-7 seconds. That makes the starch react so that the potato spaghetti becomes sticky and easier to work with.

Wrap the tubes in parchment paper and roll the spaghetti twice around each tube. Set the fryer at 180c and deep fry until crispy and golden.

Season as soon as they come out of the fryer and remove from metal tubes. It's a hot job, so be careful, but if you do not remove immediately they will get stuck.

Once cool, reserve in a dry cool place or in a dehydrator.

ROQUEFORT BUTTER

Ingredients

60g	Roquefort cheese
100g	salted butter at room temperature
	salt, pepper, cayenne and a touch of nutmeg

Method

In a food processor mix the cheese, butter and seasoning and blitz until you get a smooth consistency. Reserve in a disposable piping bag with stainless steel plain nozzle and keep at room temperature.

To assemble

Carefully fill your potatube with the Roquefort cheese butter and dip the end in finely chopped chives and serve at once.
Note: Chabichou or stilton could replace the Roquefort. Chopped roasted walnuts or hazelnuts are a delicious alternative to the chives.

CHECKERS
canapé

CORNETTO OF SMOKED SEWIN WITH LEMON CREAM AND CAVIAR

"

These canapés embrace one of Wales' most delicious ingredients – sewin.

Sewin is the UK's best sea trout and can be found in the coastal waters of Wales.

Just like asparagus and strawberries, it is a seasonal delight and it's appearance on menus means one thing: summer. Sewin is caught by coraclers who take to the water in small, round boats made from cowhide, tarred calico, willow or hazel.

Sewin fishermen have to obtain special licences, which means stocks are preserved.

The colour of the fish is a beautiful red, like the colour of wild salmon, due to its diet of shrimps and other pink-fleshed crustaceans.

Sewin has a delicious, unique taste.

"

Equipment

1 smoker (or an old tray layered with foil, a closely-fitting lid and a rack that fits inside and is propped up by 4 balls of scrunched up foil)
12 cream horns – available from good cook shops
300g oak chips

Ingredients

1	small fillet of Sewin (or wild trout)
1	neatly chopped banana shallot
5g	chopped tarragon
5g	chopped dill
5g	chopped chives
12	Feuilles de Brick (or filo pastry)
2	handfuls of rock salt
	a little bit of butter

Method – the fish mix

Run your fingers along the fish fillet, make sure there are no bones left in it. Spread some rock salt on a tray and lay the fillet on it. Cover the fillet with the remaining salt and leave it for 5 minutes. Rinse it well and pat dry. Transfer the fish onto the wire rack of the smoker. Heat up the oak chips and   when they are really smoking turn off the heat. Quickly place the wire rack with fish on top into the smoker. Close the lid and smoke/cook for about 2-4 minutes, depending on the thickness of the fillet. You have to judge when it is cooked. For instance, a thick fillet might be sufficiently smoky but not cooked through. If that is the case, finish it off in the oven at 180c for 3-5 minutes on the skin side.

Once cooked and cooled, flake the fish into a stainless steel bowl and bind with 2 spoonfuls of mayonnaise, the herbs and season with salt, pepper and cayenne. Taste and adjust the seasoning if necessary. Remember, this is the filling that will go into your cones so rectify any mistakes at this point: it will be too late once they are in the cones.

CORNETTO OF SMOKED SEWIN WITH LEMON CREAM AND CAVIAR continued

THE CONES

Method

Cut the Feuilles de Brick (or filo) into 4.

Brush them generously with the beurre pommade (soft butter) and wrap around the cream horn.

Place another cream horn on the top without pushing too hard and bake at 170c until golden brown, which should take about 8 minutes.

When cooked, take them quickly off the cream horn or they might stick to it.

Keep them in a dry place until required, or keep them in the dehydrator.

Ingredients – mayonnaise

2	egg yolks
25g	Dijon mustard
15g	white wine vinegar
225g	rapeseed oil
	salt, ground white pepper, cayenne pepper

Method

In a stainless steel bowl, whisk the egg yolks and mustard until pale in colour.

Add the vinegar, a pinch of salt, pepper and cayenne and slowly drizzle in the oil, whisking all the time.

Taste and correct the seasoning if necessary.

Store in the fridge.

Ingredients – lemon chantilly

1	grated lemon – zest and juice
200ml	double cream
	salt, pepper, cayenne to taste

Method

In a stainless steel bowl use a spatula to gently fold in all of the ingredients until you get a velvety smooth texture. Do not overbeat or use a whisk, or it will split.

Taste and rectify the seasoning and sharpness.

Reserve in a piping bag with a plain stainless steel nozzle attached.

Keep filled piping bag in fridge until ready to use.

ASSEMBLE THE DISH

Hold the cornetto's in individual shot glasses to steady.

Fill with the sewin tartare-cream.

Top up with the lemon chantilly.

Finish with Oscietra caviar.

Serve at once in a sturdy porcelain holder or in an individual tall shot glass.

61

CHECKERS
canapé

OYSTER ROLL WITH THAI DRESSING

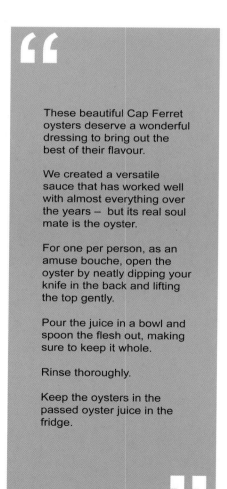

These beautiful Cap Ferret oysters deserve a wonderful dressing to bring out the best of their flavour.

We created a versatile sauce that has worked well with almost everything over the years – but its real soul mate is the oyster.

For one per person, as an amuse bouche, open the oyster by neatly dipping your knife in the back and lifting the top gently.

Pour the juice in a bowl and spoon the flesh out, making sure to keep it whole.

Rinse thoroughly.

Keep the oysters in the passed oyster juice in the fridge.

Ingredients

50g	of oyster flesh
20g	egg white
	a pinch of fine table salt and a pinch of cayenne
20cl	double cream
	pak choi leaves, blanched and julienne, to serve

Method

In a blender, blitz the oyster, egg and seasoning. Then add the double cream and blitz. Check the seasoning.

Roll the mousse in a sausage shape in cling film and poach at 55c for 15 minutes. Refresh right away in ice water.

Lay some blanched pak choi leaves over a sheet of cling film. Wrap them gently around the oyster mousse. Keep in the fridge.

To dress

On a slate, place some wet rock salt and make an indentation with a spoon. Place the clean oyster shell on the top and some thick julienne of pak choi stem inside the shell. Slice the oyster sausage at around 1.5cm and arrange the raw oyster neatly next to it. Spoon a generous amount of Thai dressing on it and decorate with a few leaves of micro coriander. Serve.

THAI DRESSING

Ingredients

12.5g	red wine vinegar
100g	soy sauce
100g	sesame oil
45g	brown sugar
	grated zest of 1 lime
2	chopped up spring onions
1	lime – grated, skin and juice
10g	finely diced ginger
1	finely diced red chilli
2g	sechuan pepper
	a few chopped leafs of coriander
5g	toasted sesame seed

Method

In a stainless steel bowl mix all of the ingredients and marinate for 2 hours before using.

TWICE BAKED SMOKED BLAENAVON CHEESE SOUFFLÉ

Yield – 10 soufflés

This is originally one of Sarah's dishes from her time as a private chef.

It has been a major hit with our guests – to the point that return visitors would order it every time they came!

We have tried it with many cheeses – but this beautiful smoked welsh cheddar from Blaenavon is certainly the best.

Although a relatively simple dish, it is easy to get wrong.

Follow the method here to the letter and you should be able to create the perfect cheese soufflé.

Equipment
Kenwood Major food mixer (or similar) with the whisk attachment

Ingredients

20g	butter
20g	flour
80g	finely grated Blaenavon Cheddar
140g	milk
2	yolks
200g	egg white
	juice of half a lemon
	soft butter to line the moulds
	grated mature cheddar to line the moulds

Method

Preheat the oven to 190c.

Butter the 10 moulds with soft butter and place in the fridge and chill for 5 minutes.

When cold, add a second layer of butter and line thoroughly with grated mature Cheddar.

Keep the moulds in the fridge.

In a saucepan, melt butter and add flour, cook for 1 minute on a moderate heat and add the milk. Bring to the boil.

When boiling, take off the heat and whisk in the grated Blaenavon cheese, salt, pepper and cayenne followed by the egg yolks.

In a Kenwood Major food mixer

with the whisk attachment, whisk the egg white and lemon juice in a meticulously clean bowl.

Beat to soft peaks.

Whisk 1/3 of the egg white into the cheese mixture. With a maryse, fold cheese mixture into remaining egg white. Do not overmix. Spoon mixture into pre-lined moulds and place in a bain-marie. Cook in preheated oven for about 10 minutes, turning the tray after 6 minutes.

The soufflés should be golden, well risen, and firm to the touch.

Remove the moulds from the bain marie and leave the soufflés to rest for 10 minutes at room temperature.

Turn out the soufflés and store on their baking dish.

Ingredients – soufflé cream

300g double cream
100g grated smoked Blaenavon cheese
salt, pepper, cayenne

Method

In a saucepan, boil the cream and take off the heat. Add the cheese and mix throughly with a whisk or hand blender.

Serving the soufflés

Preheat your oven at 200c with the fan on. Pour the soufflé cream over your soufflés and bake for approximatley 8-10 minutes, turning the tray halfway through.

Serve at once with a well-dressed salad of mixed leaves, peeled roasted almonds and dice of Granny Smith apple.

TERRINE DE POIREAUX ET FOIE GRAS FAÇON CHECKERS

Yield – Serves 8

> When we launched our restaurant, we were known as 'The Frenchman and the Farmer's Daughters'.
>
> That's because of my Gallic roots and the fact that Sarah and Kathryn were raised locally on a dairy farm.
>
> The title has stuck and at The Checkers we try to combine the best of French and Welsh food, marrying beautifully fresh, seasonal ingredients from Wales in great dishes that are rooted in French classics.
>
> Occasionally, we put the two together and this is one such example.
>
> It brings together one of France's most iconic ingredients with one of Wales' most valued ones.

Equipment

A terrine mould 9x9x20cm
Tweezers

Ingredients – the leeks

20	young leeks

Method

Cook the leeks in salted boiling water until very soft, which should take about 20 minutes. Refresh them in iced water. When cold, squeeze out as much water as possible and dry them thoroughly overnight between two clean kitchen towels.

Ingredients – foie gras

2x 500g	foie gras
14g	fine table salt
3g	ground white Pepper
3g	caster sugar
1	generous pinch of cayenne
2g	five spice
50ml	white port
50ml	Madeira

Method

Sous vide the foie gras lobes and dip in cold water for 2 hours. On a clean sanitized table, carefully de-vein 2 foie gras lobes with tweezers and a spoon.
Season with the salt, pepper, sugar and spices and drizzle the alcohol over evenly. Place the seasoned liver in a square terrine.

Cook in a waterbath at 53c for 10 minutes. Refresh in iced water.

ASSEMBLING THE TERRINE

With a knife dipped in boiling water, slice the foie gras rectangle into 3x3x20cm and store on a flat tray in the fridge. You will need five pieces.

Cling film twice the 9x9x20cm terrine mould, both along the height and the length.

Place the foie gras rectangle at the bottom right and left of each end and the leeks in the middle.

If the leeks are too small to match their allocation, open the outside and bulk it up with another until you get the desired size.

Alternate the ingredients for the second layer, with 2 leeks and 1 foie gras rectangle.

Finally alternate the ingredients again for the 3rd and final layer.

Neatly close the cling film above the terrine and place a flat tray above it with a heavy-ish weight on top, such as a 2lt plastic milk container.

Keep the finished terrine in the fridge for 24 hours before serving.

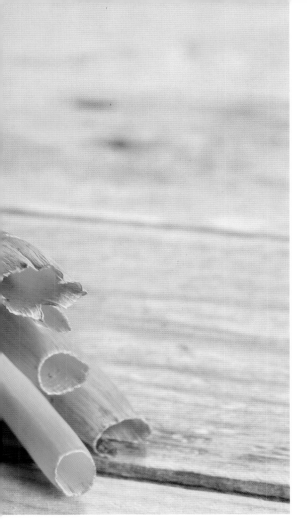

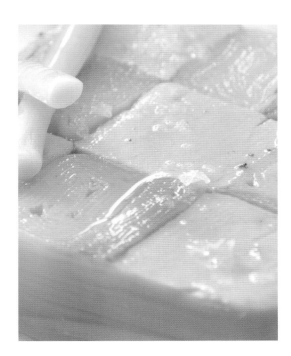

CHECKERS

TERRINE DE POIREAUX ET FOIE GRAS FAÇON CHECKERS continued

Wrapping the terrine in leeks

In a piece of cling film big enough to wrap the terrrine, layer the leeks like a rectangle to 29x20cm.

Place your leek and foie gras piece in the middle. Wrap it tightly and place it straight onto a chopping board.

Serving the terrine

With a long, sharp slicing knife, cut the terrine every 3cm along. It will be very fragile so plate it right away and brush the slice with a vinaigrette.

Garnish with cooked baby leeks and serve with toasted brioche.

PÂTÉ DE PIGEON AUX CERISES

Yield – 6 portions

> Presentation and flavour combine in this exquisite dish.
>
> If ever there was a pate that resonated with the flavours of France, then surely this is the dish.
>
> Cherry and pigeon are a perfect pairing.
>
> Coupling those with deliciously indulgent foie gras and a farce made from veal, double cream and cognac makes this dish both indulgent and memorable.
>
> Served with a fresh salad and one of our homemade breads, this dish remains a popular slice of France and is a favourite of many.

Equipment

Meat grinder
Combi oven
Blow torch

Ingredients – the pâté

1	Squab pigeon
	Generous splash of Cognac and Kirsch

Method

Delicately de-bone the pigeon from the back, removing every bone except the middle wing tips and the knee knuckle. Pay attention to remove all the sinew and fat, especially on the leg. Remove the little fillet on top of the breast and marinate the bird for 24 hours in the fridge with a generous helping of Cognac and Kirsch.

Ingredients – the farce

50g	raw foie gras	1		egg yolk
100g	diced pigeon flesh			generous splash of
100g	diced pork fat			cognac
100g	diced veal loin	10g		tarragon
100g	double cream	5g		chives

Method

Put all the meat and fat through the meat grinder and then add the egg yolk, tarragon and chives to the minced meat. Season with salt, pepper and cayenne pepper and beat in the cream, little by little. Test a little of the farce in the frying pan to check for seasoning and consistency. Keep in the fridge until needed.

On a chopping board, lay out the bird and put a small amount of farce, evenly spread, on both the breast and leg. Flash fry the foie gras to colour, season and place between the breast and place a thin layer of farce on the top. Close the pâté joining the two shoulders and two legs together using tooth picks.

PÂTÉ DE PIGEON AUX CERISES continued

Ingredients – cherries in a jar

2kg	of stoned black cherries, with stalks on
2l	red wine
200g	red wine vinegar
250g	sugar
5g	five spice
3g	salt
3	cinnamon stick
5g	black pepper
	the broken stones of 2 kilos of cherries

Method

Bring all the liquor ingredients to the boil. Add the cherries and bring back to a light simmer.

Take off the stove and leave to cook with a residual heat.

Once cold, place the cherries in a Kilner jar, pass the liquor through a sieve, pour over the cherries and store the jar in the fridge.

starter

CHERRY KETCHUP

Ingredients

240g	black cherry puree
75g	port reduced to 40g
25g	boiled Cabernet Sauvignon vinegar
10g	boiled balsamic vinegar
1g	salt
3g	agar agar

Method

Bring all the ingredients, except the agar agar, to 80c respectous of any further boiling and reducing.

Add the agar agar and cook until it reaches 95c.

Once set, blitz in a tall blender until really smooth then pass through a fine mesh, conical sieve and keep in a squeezy bottle.

COOKING THE PATE

In a Rational oven, cook at 63c for 2 hours.

Once cooked, brown all sides with a blow torch.

Cool and rest in a fridge until needed.

HOME SMOKED TOMATO SOUP, DRIED BLACK OLIVE, GOAT'S CHEESE QUENELLE

Yield — 6-8 portions

> A glut of tomatoes was the inspiration for this soup.
>
> We were inundated one summer and wanted to find a way to put their sweet, summery flavours to use.
>
> The soup was incredibly well received, so much so that we offered it at a pop up restaurant when invited to the Ludlow Food Festival.
>
> It proved incredibly popular with guests, who were disappointed that it was not available outside of summer.
>
> It has a great smoky, sweet flavour that is well balanced by the chalky coarseness of the goat's cheese.
>
> It can be used as a coulis, for instance, with octopus (see page 124), or as a garnish for grilled artichokes.

Equipment

Dehydrator (or low oven)
Home smoker
Oak chips
Oak dust
Tall jug food processor

Ingredients — olive crumb

200g whole black olives

Method

Lay the olives on a sheet of baking parchment and semi-dry in the dehydrator (or a very low oven) for about 6 hours at 68c. Once squishy, chop to the size of a peppercorn with a knife and reserve in a dry place.

When semi-dried take them out and keep them in a dark dry place or they will become too dry.

Ingredients — the goat's cheese quenelle

1.5g	Agar agar
50g	milk
100g	Chabichou goat's cheese log with skin on
	salt, pepper and cayenne

Method

Season the milk with salt, pepper, cayenne pepper and bring to 80c. Add the agar agar. Whisk meticulously and bring to 98c. Then add the goat's cheese dice and transfer to a tray. Cool in the blast chiller or fridge. Once set and cold, blitz in a tall jug food processor and pass it through fine mesh tamis.

Reserve in the fridge.

HOME SMOKED TOMATO SOUP, DRIED BLACK OLIVE, GOAT'S CHEESE QUENELLE continued

Ingredients – the soup

80g	butter
350g	finely sliced onions
25g	crushed garlic clove
2	sprigs of thyme
1400g	tomatoes on the vine
80g	tomato paste
250g	chicken or vegetable stock
250g	double cream
	salt, pepper, cayenne and sugar to taste

Method

In a large, heavy-bottomed pan, melt the butter and gently sweat the garlic, onions and thyme for 1 hour, until translucent.

While the onions are slowly cooking, cut all the tomatoes in 2. One half will be roasted while the other will be smoked.

Smoke half of the fruit with two handfuls of oak chips and 1 handful of oak dust. Smoke for about 45 minutes. Leave to cool on the rack.

In the oven at 170c and on a well olive-oiled-tray, roast the remaining tomatoes.

Drizzle with olive oil and seasoning until well cooked, which should take 40 minutes. Once cooked, keep on the tray.

When the onions and garlic are well cooked, add all the tomatoes, smoked and roasted, the tomato paste, chicken stock and cream and simmer for 5 minutes. Blitz in the tall blender and pass through a conical sieve. Adjust the seasoning and correct the balance with caster sugar if too acidic.

Reserve in the fridge. The soup will mature and the flavours will become much more pronounced the next day and even better the day after that.

MARINATED TOMATO GARNISH

Ingredients

40	cherry tomatoes, using 5 marinated cherry tomatoes per bowl of soup
25ml	balsamic vinegar
75ml	olive oil
15g	caster sugar
6g	salt
2g	ground white pepper
3g	crushed garlic cloves
2	sprigs of thyme, the leaves only

Method

In a pan of boiling water, dip the criss-crossed tomatoes for about 12 seconds (keep the water boiling at all times), and refresh straight away in ice-water.

With a hand blender, mix the balsamic vinegar, olive oil, sugar, salt, pepper and garlic then add the thyme leaves.

Correct the seasoning if necessary and reserve.

Peel the tomato and marinate them in the balsamic dressing for 30 minutes. Lay the cherry tomatoes on a piece of greaseproof paper and place in the dehydrator for 6 hours and reserve in a dry cool place.

To serve

Scatter a few oven-dried cherry tomatoes at the bottom of the warmed soup bowl and pour the hot soup over them. With 2 large spoons, quenelle some goat cream in the middle and sprinkle a neat line of dried olives across the top.

VELOUTE DE PERSIL PLAT, CUISSES DE GRENOUILLES POCHEES, CAPPUCCINO A L AIL CONFIT

Yield – 4-5 portions

"

This is an unusual soup – but we absolutely love it.

It's a parsley veloute with poached frogs' legs and a garlic cappuccino.

The parsley flavour is Kathryn's favourite and the dish is beautifully balanced.

Guests are continually surprised at the depth and fine flavour of this dish and for many of them, it's the first time they've eaten frogs' legs.

Equipment
Sous vide machine
Bamix hand blender

Ingredients – the veloute

20g	butter
200g	sliced white onions
50g	leeks
50g	red washed potatoes
1l	chicken stock
350g	picked flat parsley leaf, 1 very large bunch
125g	raw washed French spinach
175g	double cream

Method

Sweat the onions with the butter until golden and translucent.

Add the leeks and the diced potatoes and sweat for another minute.

Add the chicken stock and simmer for 10 minutes.

While the base is simmering, bring a deep pan to the boil and dip the parsley and the spinach into it, little by little for 30 seconds at a time.

The water must be boiling continually to cook the chlorophyll.

Refresh right away in an ice bath.

Drain the parsley and spinach well and add to the base and simmer for a further 5 minutes.

Add the cream and simmer for a further 5 minutes.

Blitz in the food blender and pass through a conical sieve.

Season and refresh as quickly as possible.

Ingredients – poached frogs' legs

Rock Salt
8 frogs legs

Method

Salt the frogs' legs for 20 minutes in rock salt.

Rinse them thoroughly and sous vide in the water bath for 1 hour at 63c.

Refresh the frogs' leg bag in ice water and once cold open the bag.

Pick through the legs and remove the bones and cartilage.

Place the meat in the fridge.

Ingredients – Garlic Cappuccino

100g	double cream
200g	semi-skimmed milk
2	garlic cloves
6	leaves gelatine
	salt
	pepper

Method

Put the gelatine in a bowl of cold water.

In a saucepan, bring the seasoned milk, cream and garlic to about 80c.

Add the soft gelatine and keep warm. Have a Bamix hand blender at the ready.

Serve the veloute

Flake the frogs' legs at the bottom of your warmed, coffee cup; we use see through for a dramatic effect.

Pour the hot soup at 90c, leaving a gap on the top for the foam to rest. Froth up the garlic cappuccino with the hand blender and spoon it on the top of each cup.

Serve at once.

STUFFED COURGETTE FLOWER WITH ROASTED SCOTTISH LANGOUSTINE, LANGOUSTINE CREAM AND CHIVE OIL

Yield – 6 portions

This pretty dish appears in the restaurant at the start of spring, when the courgette flowers are blossoming and langoustines are aplenty.

The balance of flavours is majestic and it's a light dish, with the scallop mousse and langoustine being ably supported by the young courgette.

We order them straight from small fishing boats in Scotland and they arrive alive and very snappy.

They are placed in the blast freezer for 10 minutes, which humanely kills them.

Equipment

Food blender
Hand held thermometer

Ingredients – the langoustines

6   langoustines (frozen for 10 minutes)

Method

Split the body from the head of the dead langoustine and castrate the tails by twisting the middle of the tail and pulling the intestinal tube out.

Once done, stick them straight together, one against the other, and tie them up with a piece of string. This is simply to achieve a straight shape.

Ingredients – court bouillon

2lt   water
1   roughly diced carrot
1   peeled and chopped onion
           a bouquet garni
           a dash of vinegar

Method

Bring all of the ingredients to the boil and blanch the tied-up langoustines for 30 seconds.

Refresh right away in an ice bath.

Once cold, with a pair of sharp scissors delicately remove the outer shell leaving only the very end of the tail for presentation purposes.

Store them carefully between 2 new j cloths, in the fridge.

STUFFED COURGETTE FLOWER WITH ROASTED SCOTTISH LANGOUSTINE, LANGOUSTINE CREAM AND CHIVE OIL continued

Ingredients – the langoustine sauce

40g	butter
20	langoustine heads
3	medium peeled, chopped banana shallots
8	sliced button mushrooms
100g	brandy
200g	white wine
30g	tomato puree
100g	fresh, roughly diced tomatoes
400g	fish stock
1	large sprig of tarragon
1	large sprig of thyme
2	bay leaves
400g	double cream
125g	salted butter

Method

In a large pan, melt the butter and lightly colour the mushrooms and shallots.

Add the langoustine heads and cook for a further minute. Add the brandy and reduce until syrupy. Add the white wine and reduce by half.

Add the tomato puree, fresh tomatoes, fish stock, tarragon, thyme and bay leaves and simmer gently until reduced by half.

Pour in the cream and reduce by half again. When ready, pass the sauce through a moulis to extract as much juice as possible and then through a conical sieve to get rid of all the pieces of shell.

Add the fresh diced butter and combine with a hand blender. Adjust the seasoning, being generous with the cayenne as it tastes much better with a kick.

Reserve until ready to use.

Ingredients – chive oil

30g	of roughly chopped chives
250ml	olive oil
	salt

Method

In the pan and over a stove, use the hand held thermometer to bring the oil to 60c.

Pour into a running food blender with the chives already in it. Add a pinch of salt and let it run for a minute.

Pass right away through a conical sieve lined with a muslin cloth in a bowl over ice to prevent it going brown.

Once cold, store in the fridge in a squeezy bottle until required.

Ingredients – scallop mousse

100g	fresh scallops
30g	egg white
100g	double cream
	table salt
	ground white pepper
	a pinch of cayenne

Method

In a tall blender, blitz the scallop, the egg white and seasoning until a silky smooth puree is obtained.

Carefully add the cream while the blender is still running and stop as soon as a thick, homogenised puree is realised. Pass through a fine sieve and adjust the seasoning if necessary. Store in a disposable piping bag and keep in the fridge.

SEASONING TRAY

At the Checkers we like to keep a seasoning tray at hand in every section.

It saves a lot of time because it has all of the things that we habitually need:

- fine table salt
- ground white pepper
- cayenne pepper
- a pot of caster sugar
- ground nutmeg
- sliced lemon
- chopped garlic cloves
- thyme

Ingredients – the courgette flower

6	courgette flowers
1	baby gem
80g	butter
	Maldon sea salt
	Micro amaranth

Method

With a sharp, serrated knife make 5 incisions into the courgette making sure the flower remains attached.

Very gently open the courgette flower and remove the stamen.

Fill with the well-seasoned scallop mousse and lay on a perforated gastronome tray.

Cook and assemble

Organisation is key, and once the courgettes are in the oven you have 8 minutes to dress the plate so make sure you have all your equipment – water with salt, seasoning, your non-stick pan, a pair of tongs and your diced butter.

Put the courgette flower tray in a steam oven (Rational) at 85c, full steam for 8 minutes.

Turn up the heat under a non-stick frying pan and season with salt.

Pan roast the langoustine gently for about 1 minute on each side. While that is on, heat the langoustine sauce.

Finish the langoustines with a knob of fresh butter.

Once just about cooked and golden, take them out and lay them on absorbent paper to get rid of the unwanted fat.

Dip the baby gem for 10 seconds in water and place next to the langoustines.

On warm plate, lay the cooked courgette flowers on the buttered baby gem and arrange the langoustines nicely on the top.

Correct the sauce for seasoning and whizz it with the hand blender to get a bubbly effect.

Spoon the langoustine foam above the crustacean and pour it around attractively.

Squeeze some chive oil around and brush the courgette flower with olive oil and sprinkle with Maldon sea salt.

Scatter a few micro-amaranth and serve at once.

ROASTED SCOTTISH SCALLOPS, CRAB & TOMATO CANNELLONI, FENNEL SHAVINGS AND SAUCE VIERGE

Yield – 6 portions

We get the most wonderful large diver scallops from Scotland and amazing cock crabs from Devon.

The cannelloni is made with the juiciest Marmande tomato.

Combined, these ingredients truly make this dish summer on a plate.

Equipment

Dehydrator
Benriner mandolin

Ingredients – the scallops

6	extra-large scallops

Method

With a sharp boning knife, carefully scrape open the lid of the live scallops.

With a spoon, gently scoop out the flesh and discard the shell.

Placing your fingers between the skirt and the flesh, deftly pull the skirt away leaving the flesh intact.

Wash the flesh thoroughly and keep in the fridge.

Ingredients – the tomato consommé

2kg	roughly cut marmande tomatoes
150g	white wine
30g	roughly chopped parsley
30g	chopped chervil
15g	chopped tarragon
15g	chopped basil
15g	chopped dill
1	roughly chopped banana shallot
1	crushed garlic clove
1	big sprig of thyme
	fine salt
	ground white pepper to taste
	caster sugar

Method

In a big stainless steel bowl, mix all the above ingredients and marinate for 48 hours.

Then hang in a muslin cloth and leave suspended over a large bowl overnight. Adjust the seasoning if necessary.

Ingredients – the tomato sheets

Place a straight stainless steel tray, in the fridge and weigh all your ingredients.

200g	tomato consommé
1.7g	agar powder

Method

Bring 100g of consommé and the agar just beneath the boil and add the remaining tomato stock. Whisk meticulously.

Tip the contents on the cold tray and make sure it stays flat. The jelly needs to be around 1mm thick. When set, cut a 4cmx3cm rectangle shape with a knife and set aside on baking parchment in the fridge.

ROASTED SCOTTISH SCALLOPS, CRAB & TOMATO CANNELLONI, FENNEL SHAVINGS AND SAUCE VIERGE continued

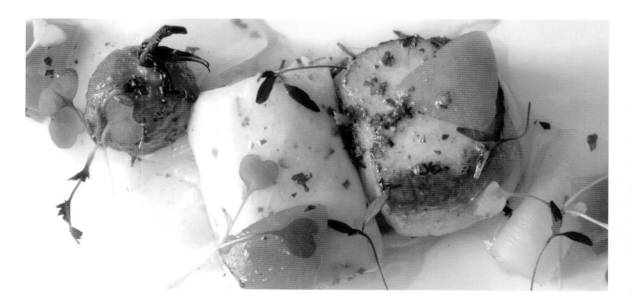

THE CRAB

Ingredients

1	cock crab
2	roughly chopped carrots
1	large diced onion
	thyme sprigs
	bay leaf
	dash of vinegar

Method

Place the live crab in the freezer for 1 hour. Put a large pan of water to boil. When boiling, submerge the crab and boil for 20 minutes. Refresh right away in ice water.

When cold, detach the claws and break them up with a kitchen hammer.

Pick through the white meat. Repeat the operation with the leg. Crab goes off very quickly so work a small batch at a time, especially when picking.

Pick through the white crab meat and keep in the fridge.

Ingredients – mayonnaise

30g	egg yolks
25g	Dijon mustard
225g	vegetable oil
15g	white wine vinegar
2g	fine salt
1	pinch ground white pepper
1	pinch cayenne

Method

Whisk the yolks, vinegar, mustard and the salt and pepper and slowly trickle the oil over it. When light and homogenous, check and correct the seasoning if necessary. Transfer to a container and keep in the fridge.

Ingredients – the tomato and crab cannelloni

5g	chopped basil leaves
5g	of diced tarragon
60g	white crab meat
2	spoons of mayonnaise, just enough to bind
15g	lemon juice
4g	grated lemon rind

Method

Bind all the above ingredients together. Season. Place the crab mix on the tomato jelly sheets and close them securely and neatly. Repeat the operation with all of the crab and sheets and keep in the fridge.

Ingredients – the aged tomatoes

12	cherry tomato on the vine
1	thinly sliced garlic clove
10ml	balsamic vinegar
30cl	olive oil
1	sprig of thyme (leaves only)
	fine salt and ground white pepper

Method

With a serrated knife, criss-cross the tomatoes and dip them in boiling water for 12 seconds.

Refresh in iced water straight away.

Peel them and mix them with all the other ingredients.

Put them on a dehydrator tray previously laid with some parchment paper. Leave in dehydrator (or low oven) for 6 hours at 59c.

When ready, take them out and store them in an air tight container. Keep them dry.

Ingredients – cooked fennel seed

1	small handful of fennel seed

Method

Place the fennel seeds in a pan alongside some water and cook gently until super soft. This will take anywhere between 1 and 3 hours depending on how dry the seeds are.

Ingredients the sauce vierge

10	cherry tomatoes
50g	lemon juice
200ml	olive oil
6g	ground coriander
	fine salt
	ground white pepper
25g	basil

Method

Blowtorch the cherry tomatoes and once the skin is loose dip them in cold water. Peel, quarter and de-seed and discard seed. Cut the quarters in half, leaving you with pretty tomato triangles. Pat dry and keep in the fridge. Place all the other ingredients in a pan. Chop 25g basil into julienne and reserve in the fridge.

TO ASSEMBLE

Heat a non-stick frying pan on medium heat and with a Benriner mandolin slice 1 head of fennel very thinly into a stainless steel bowl.

Season the fennel with lime juice, olive oil, some cooked fennel seeds and a few bits of pickled ginger (recipe page 104) and salt and pepper.

Squeeze some olive oil in the hot pan, season and roast the scallop with the biggest side facing down. Cook it for about 1 minute, add a knob of salted butter and take it off the heat. Turn the scallops over and keep cooking in the butter using the residual heat of the pan.

When barely warm in the middle (check with a skewer) transfer them on a wire rack and keep warm. Heat up the oil and lemon juice mix for the vierge sauce. Correct the seasoning and add the cherry tomato triangle. Keep warm.

On a rectangle plate, using a square cutter, place the well-seasoned fennel shaving in the middle. Place the cannelloni on top, slightly aside, and the warm roasted scallop on the other.

Place the aged tomato on the side of the scallop. Add the basil julienne to the warm sauce and pour on the plates. Finish with a few micro leaves. Serve.

CHECKERS
vegetarian

PETITS LÉGUMES OUBLIÉS A'LA TRUFFE NOIRE

Yield – 6 small le parfait jars

> This is one of my favourite Winter accompaniments of all time.
>
> It's like a soup in a jar with all the different flavours of root vegetables kept together and enhanced with a decadent black truffle flavour.
>
> It is absolutely exceptional and incredibly easy to do.
>
> We have used it with beef, lamb and occasionally with oxtail-stuffed, line-caught turbot.

Ingredients – Jerusalem artichoke

12	peeled medium Jerusalem artichokes
250ml	cream
250ml	milk
	salt
	pepper

Method

In a hot saucepan, bring the milk and cream to the boil and season to taste.

Submerge the artichokes and poach in the oven for 45-60 minutes at 160c.

Check from time to time as the cooking time can vary.

When cooked and still with a bite, leave to cool in the liquid.

Ingredients – Jerusalem artichoke veloute

50g	good quality salted butter
300g	finely sliced onions
6	cooked Jerusalem artichoke (recipe above)
50g	vegetable stock all the cream and milk from the cooking of the artichokes

Method

On a very low heat, slowly confit the sliced onions in the butter, which will take 90-120 minutes.

When completely, cooked and beautifully sweet add the cooked Jerusalem artichokes, quickly followed by the stock.

Bring to the boil and add the milk and cream and boil again.

Transfer to a tall blender and blitz till you get a velvety like sauce.

Pass through a conical sieve and transfer to a container and keep in the fridge.

Ingredients – celeriac

300g	celeriac
	salted water

Method

Peel celeriac and dice 12 pieces of 2x2 cm celeriac chunks, making them slightly irregular to give them a rustic look.

Poach in salted, simmering water until cooked but still with a bite.

When ready cool in iced water.

Ingredients – carrots

3	carrots
400g	water
75g	sugar
150g	butter
	salt to taste
1	sprig of thyme and
1	bayleaf

Method

Peel the carrots and slice them quite thick, 0.8cm, at an angle. Cook them thoroughly, but with a bite, in a light syrup made up from the other ingredients.

Ingredients – chestnut

30	chestnuts
	table salt

Method

With a small serrated kitchen knife, score and wrap

30 fresh chestnuts in a papillotte of aluminium foil and bake over salt in an oven set at 180c.

Peel the tough outer skin and sous vide them all together.

Finish in a sous vide at 75c for 4hours.

Refresh in iced water and keep in the bag until needed or alternatively buy some peeled, ready to serve chestnuts.

Ingredients – black truffle

6	medium Perigord black truffles

Assemble dish

Heat up the velouté and split among the jars.

Now drain, dry and divide all the vegetables equally between the jars – there is no real order as long as everybody gets a truffle.
Put in steamer for 5-7 minutes and serve at once.

CHECKERS
vegetarian

GRILLED GLOBE ARTICHOKE, AUBERGINE PURÉE, MELTED GOAT'S CHEESE & PESTO

Yield – 8 portions

> "One of the very first vegetarian dishes we served at the Herbert Arms helped to shape the future of our business.
>
> It was reviewed by Sophie Bignall, a food critic at the Shropshire Star newspaper.
>
> She gave it a 5-star review, which gave us a huge boost.
>
> Our morale soared and it reassured us that we were on the right track.
>
> If you prepare the artichoke from scratch, you may as well do all 12 of them as they are delicious in a purée or in salads with a lemon and black olive dressing."

Equipment

Tall jug blender

Ingredients – artichoke

There is a saying in France that you are a good chef if you can: beautifully chop shallots, make a well-seasoned plump omelette and turn artichokes.

Such skills are not easily gained and require pig-headedness to do well. A plain, razor-sharp knife for the shallots and a small, new serrated one for the final turning are a big help.

3l	water
750ml	white wine
600ml	olive oil
1 head	of garlic chopped in half
2	celery stalks
125g	sea salt
25g	ground black pepper
1	bouquet of thyme and bay leaves (bouquet garni)
12	large artichokes Breton
2	lemons

Method

In a pan, mix the water, white wine, olive oil, garlic, celery, salt, pepper and bouquet garni. Put to one side as this will be your cooking liquor.

Cut lemon in half and squeeze juice out in a large stainless steel bowl. Break the tail of the globe artichoke and break and pull 2-3 layers of the outer leaves.

With a serrated kitchen knife, work your way through the tough outer green in a turning motion over a chopping board ensuring not to come too close to the flesh.

With a small, sharp serrated knife, turn until you have a neat, uniform artichoke heart.

Leave the choke in, as they are much easier to remove once the artichokes are cooked. Make sure to trim well around it.

Cover artichokes in lemon juice as you go along, to prevent oxidisation.

Heat the liquor and when boiling, submerge the artichoke and lemon in the pan. Cover with a sheet of baking parchment and boil for 10 minutes.

Once cooked, leave at room temperature to cool in the liquor for 12 hours. When cold, transfer the artichoke to a plastic box with a lid and pass the liquor over it through a conical sieve.

Keep refrigerated until needed.

91

AUBERGINE PURÉE

Ingredients

3	large aubergines
20g	chopped garlic
	cumin powder
3	large sprigs of thyme and bay leaf
	fine salt and ground white pepper
150ml	cream reduced to 90g

Method

Lay the aubergines on 2 layers of kitchen foil and top and tail them. Cut in 2 lengthways and criss-cross the flesh with a small serrated knife.

Spread the chopped garlic evenly between them, dust with a generous amount of cumin powder and add thyme and bay leaves as well as fine salt and pepper.

Roll the aubergine in the foil and bake at 180c for 2-3 hours. When cooked, open the foil and discard the thyme and bay leaves.

Scoop all the flesh and half of the skin into a tall blender. Blitz and gradually add the warm reduced double cream until a nice purée consistency is obtained. Season and refrigerate.

GRILLED GLOBE ARTICHOKE, AUBERGINE PURÉE, MELTED GOAT'S CHEESE & PESTO continued

Ingredients – pesto

This versatile Italian dressing is incredibly useful for all sorts of situations. When Sarah was on the canape section at the Waterside Inn, she came up with an anchovy and pesto croute which we use at The Checkers as one of our regular canapés.

4g	crushed garlic
50g	lightly coloured pine kernels
75g	grated parmesan
300ml	olive oil
75g	freshly picked basil leaves
	fine table salt, ground white pepper

Method

In the mixer attachment from a Braun 750w, whizz the garlic, pine kernels and 100g of oil. Pulse intermittently until you get a rough texture. Add the basil and blitz a little more, again, leaving it quite rough.

Transfer to a stainless steel bowl and fold in the grated parmesan and the remaining oil. Season with salt and ground white pepper and keep in a plastic container with lid in the fridge.

Ingredients – goat's cheese discs

100g   goat's cheese log

Method

Trim the skin off the goat's tranche and slice. Place between 2 sheets of cling film. Using a rolling pin, roll it to a 2mm thickness and keep on a tray in the fridge.

Ingredients – lemon zest confit

20g	lemon skin (no pith)
100g	sugar
	water as needed

Method

With a plain sharp knife, julienne the lemon skin neatly and transfer it to a pan of cold water and bring to the boil. When boiling, refresh right away and repeat the operation 2 more times. Make a syrup of 100g sugar and 100g water and bring to the boil. When boiling put the blanched lemon skin in and confit until cooked and flavourful, which should take 2-3 hours. When ready, keep in a plastic box with a lid on in the fridge.

TO ASSEMBLE

Turn on the gas under the cast iron griddle pan and turn on the grill. Heat up some of the passed cooking liquor from the artichoke in a pan and have a baking tray at the ready.

With a spoon, delicately pull the artichoke hair out, discard, and dip in the simmering liquor for 3 minutes. In a small pan, heat up the aubergine puree. Warm up the pesto in a skillet.

Cut 4 goat's cheese discs neatly with a plain 9cm cutter. Pull the artichoke out using a pair of tongs and place on the tray.

Season and roll in olive oil. Griddle the 4 warm artichokes about 4 seconds on each side and put back on the tray.

Fill up the cavity with some warm, seasoned aubergine puree and top up with a goat's cheese disc. Scatter a few panko breadcrumbs on. Place under the grill until golden. Lay 4 warm plates in front of you and put 1 artichoke on each of them. Spoon the warm pesto on and around and scatter a few roasted pine nuts on top.

Finish with warm confit of lemon julienne. Serve.

CHECKERS
vegetarian

GIROLLES AU VINAIGRE

"

This is a brilliant recipe for pickling girolles, which make a stunning accompaniment for terrine and foie gras mi-cuit.

Leave them to mature in the sweet and sour brine for a couple of weeks before using them.

Prior to pickling, prepare the jars.

To sterilise the jars place in the oven for 15 minutes at 140c or boil in a large pan of water for 15 minutes.

It is imperative that the jars are sterilised thoroughly.

"

Ingredients

500g	clean girolles with the stalks scrapped
250g	of clear honey
50g	white wine vinegar
25g	whole coriander seed
12	capsules of green cardammon

Method

Place the raw mushrooms inside the sterilised jar.

In a large pan, bring the honey to a light colour caramel and deglaze with the vinegar and spices.

Pour it over the mushrooms and close the lid.

CHECKERS
vegetarian

TRANCHE DE GRATIN DAUPHINOIS, SAUCE BÉCHAMEL AU ROQUEFORT, SALADE A LA MOUTARDE

Yield – 4-6 portions

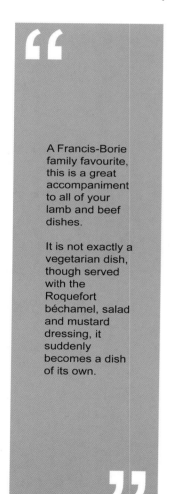

"

A Francis-Borie family favourite, this is a great accompaniment to all of your lamb and beef dishes.

It is not exactly a vegetarian dish, though served with the Roquefort béchamel, salad and mustard dressing, it suddenly becomes a dish of its own.

"

Equipment

2	le Creuset, terrine-shaped moulds
1	roll of baking parchment

Ingredients – Gratin

To achieve a tranche effect, make sure you have 2 replica dishes that sit perfectly on top of each other without leaving any gap.

400ml	double cream
400ml	whole milk
30g	peeled garlic cloves
20g	thyme (leaves only)
10	peeled and thinly sliced (1.5mm) waxy potatoes such as Charlotte or Desiree varieties
	fine table salt
	ground white pepper
	ground nutmeg

Method

Using a pastry brush, butter the le Creuset dish and trim the baking parchment to fit perfectly inside.

Butter the paper.

Bring the milk, cream, garlic and thyme leaves to the boil and blitz thoroughly.

Season with salt, ground pepper and a generous helping of ground nutmeg.

Place the potatoes inside the dish.

Build the gratin in an organised and tidy fashion, placing the biggest slices to the bottom and sides.

Fill level by level, seasoning the potatoes with salt and pouring a generous ladle of milky garlic cream between each layer.

When the terrine is ¾ full, pour 2 generous ladles of milky garlic cream on top of the potatoes and close the paper neatly onto them.

Bake at 180c for 45-60 minutes.

If it gets dark too quickly, lay a piece of foil onto the gratin while cooking.

A good professional trick is to insert a skewer in the middle of the terrine to check that it's cooked: only slight resistance should occur.

When ready, remove from the oven and press the replica terrine mould on top.

Place in the fridge with a weight on top.

Rest for 24 hours.

TRANCHE DE GRATIN DAUPHINOIS, SAUCE BÉCHAMEL AU ROQUEFORT, SALADE A LA MOUTARDE continued

Ingredients – the mustard dressing

30g	Dijon mustard
20g	white wine vinegar
40g	warm water
3g	salt
1g	cayenne pepper
160g	vegetable oil
2g	ground white peppercorn

Method

In a stainless steel bowl, combine the mustard, vinegar, warm water, salt, pepper and cayenne and whisk until homogenous.

As though making a mayonnaise, slowly add the oil and emulsify. Taste and store in a squeezy bottle in the fridge.

Ingredients – Roquefort béchamel

Make this recipe 15 minutes before serving.

20g	butter
15g	white flour
130ml	milk
	fine table salt
	ground white pepper
	ground nutmeg
60g	Roquefort cheese

Method

In a saucepan, melt the butter and add the flour. Cook for 1 minute and add the milk. Bring to the boil, whisking from time to time.

Add salt, pepper, cayenne and finally the Roquefort in chunks. Whisk well but leave a few Roquefort bits for later. Cover with a cartouche as the béchamel will dry straight away and a skin will form on top. Keep warm.

TO DRESS

When cold and well pressed, pull the baking parchment and tip the terrine over on a chopping board. With a long sharp serrated knife slice the terrine lengthways, about 1.5 cm thick. Trim the extremities for that neat and sharp look.

Place on a piece of baking parchment on an oven tray. Heat in an oven set at 180c for 12-15 minutes.

Put a selection of micro salad in a stainless steel bowl and season with the mustard dressing. Lay 4 warm plates in front of you and using a long spatula place the gratin slice neatly on the plate.

Dress the salad next to it and serve the béchamel on a side dish. If the béchamel is too stiff add a bit of warm milk just before sending.

HOUSE DRESSING

Ingredients

30g	English mustard
30g	Dijon mustard
20g	salt
7g	ground white peppercorn
375ml	vegetable oil
250ml	olive oil
50g	chopped parsley
40g	roughly chopped shallots

Method

Mix all the ingredients together and marinate for 48 hours. Pass through a fine mesh conical sieve and keep in a kilner jar in the fridge. Emulsify with a hand blender before pouring into a squeezy bottle for service.

LEMON & GARLIC VINAIGRETTE

Ingredients

60g	olive oil
20g	fresh lemon juice
15g	white wine vinegar
4g	castor sugar
3g	cooking salt
1g	ground white peppercorn
1.5g	lemon zest
1.5g	garlic clove
1	sprig of thyme leaves only

Method

Mix all the ingredients together and with a 750w Braun hand blender emulsify.

Keep in a squeezy bottle in the fridge.

ROQUEFORT DRESSING

Ingredients

125g	Roquefort cheese
25g	chardonnay vinegar
60g	sour cream
50g	warm water
5g	extra virgin olive oil
1g	cayenne pepper

Method

In the plastic Robo Coupe from a Braun Hand Blender beat the cheese until it is very smooth. Gradually incorporate the vinegar. Add the sour cream until the consistency is smooth. Add the warm water, cayenne and olive oil until the desired consistency is achieved. Store in a squeezy bottle in the fridge.

ROASTED MONKFISH TAIL WITH SMOKED BACON, ROQUEFORT AND RED WINE SAUCE

Yield – 8 portions

We love monkfish.

Its meaty texture and strong flavour mean it's sufficiently robust to work with accompaniments like a strong cheese and smoked bacon.

A great wine sauce completes this dish.

Monkfish fillet and veal stock are available in good supermarkets.

Equipment

Food processor
Sous vide machine
Thermometer probe

Ingredients – the fish

4   x 200g monkfish fillet

Method

Lay the monkfish fillet on a board and trim off the skin, which pulls off like a sock.

Also remove the brown sinew. Run you finger along it to make sure there are no bones left in.

With a sharp knife neatly cut into 140g portions.

Reserve in the fridge.

Ingredients – the sauce

1.5l   red wine
375ml   red port
500ml   fish stock
500ml   veal stock
6   finely chopped shallots

Method

Reduce all the above ingredients to a sauce like consistency and pass through a conical sieve.

Ingredients – Roquefort mousse

250g	diced raw chicken breast
30g	egg white
	salt, pepper, cayenne
50g	double cream
120g	Roquefort cheese
16	rashers of thinly sliced smoked streaky bacon

Method

In a food processor, blitz the chicken breast with the egg white, salt, pepper and cayenne to a fine paste. Add the cream and the cheese and use the pulse button to homogenise the mixture. When smooth reserve in a piping bag in the fridge.

Wrap the fish

On a flat surface, place a double layer of cling film. Pipe about 80g of Roquefort mousse on it and with a small spatula spread over a rectangle big enough to wrap the fish tail completely.

Season the fish tail and delicately roll the cling film around it, tying knots on each ends that are not too loose and not too tight.

Repeat operation for each one.

When each fillet is wrapped, pre-cook in a thermocirculator for 20 minutes at 63c. Refresh straight away in ice water.

On a flat surface lay a sheet of cling film and neatly arrange rashers of thinly sliced smoked streaky bacon. Place the pre-cooked fish and mousse in the middle and wrap it tightly.

Repeat with the others and store in the fridge until needed.

When the fish is cold remove the cling film.

THE LENTILS

Ingredients

150g	puy lentils, soaked in water overnight
60g	finely chopped onions
15g	chopped garlic
80g	neatly diced carrots
80g	celery
1	large sprig of thyme and bay leaves
500ml	chicken stock

Method

In a large saucepan, sweat the onions and garlic with a knob of butter for 5 minutes.

Add the carrots and celery and cook for a further 3 minutes. When slightly roasted, add the lentils followed by the chicken stock, thyme and bay leaves, which should be tied together with a piece of kitchen string.

Simmer for 1 ½ hours, stirring occasionally. Taste for texture and seasoning and correct accordingly.

Keep in the fridge until needed.

ROASTED MONKFISH TAIL WITH SMOKED BACON, ROQUEFORT AND RED WINE SAUCE continued

To assemble

Set your oven to 190c. Drizzle some olive oil in an oven-friendly, non-stick frying pan and heat it up.

Place the fish where the bacon seal ends and gently sear it, to create a sealing effect.

Bake the fish in the pan in the pre-heated oven for 3 minutes on each of the four sides: a total of 12 minutes.

While cooking the fish, re-heat the lentils and the sauce.

Insert the tip of a thermometer probe into the fish and make sure it reaches 45c.

Leave it to rest for 5 minutes – the residual heat will carry on cooking the fish gently.

On warm plates, place the hot lentils. With a sharp serrated knife, trim the end of the fish parcel until you get to the fish fillet.

Slice 1 thick piece, 1.5cm per portion. Place on the top of the lentils.

CHECKERS
shellfish

NATIVE LOBSTER "MULLEN"

Yield – 4 portions

I designed this recipe while working as a private chef for the Mullen Family, in Cirencester.

They had a very keen interest in cooking and had fabulous taste. They were a joy to cook for.

They came to dine with us at The Checkers when we first opened and were very complimentary, which gave us a real boost.

We remain thankful.

Equipment

Benriner Mandolin
Vegetable juicer

Ingredients – lobster

4	x 500g native lobster
2	carrots
1	large onion
1	sprig of thyme
	dash of white wine vinegar
4	litres of water

Method

In a large, deep pan, make a court bouillon with 2 carrots, 1 large onion, a sprig of thyme, 4 litres of water and a dash of white wine vinegar and bring to the boil. With kitchen string, tie a wooden spoon around the lobster tail to keep it straight. It is a good idea to pop the lobsters into the freezer for 10 minutes prior to cooking.

Dip the lobster in and boil for 7 minutes. Refresh right away in iced water. When completely cold, pull the tail off and break the claws and knuckles in a tray.

With a pair of sharp scissors, carefully cut the head and tail for presentation and keep aside. Free the tail, claws and knuckles from the shell and keep in the fridge on a clean j cloth to absorb excess water.

Ingredients – pickled ginger

500g	peeled and very thinly sliced ginger root (on a Benriner Mandolin)
1	lemon, halved

Method

Put the ginger in a deep, large pan and cover with cold water and half a lemon. Bring to the boil and refresh straight away in ice water. Repeat the operation twice, changing the lemon every time to stop the ginger from discolouring. When blanched 3 times, make a syrup with:

100g	sugar
200g	of water
25cl	lemon juice

On a low heat, lightly confit ginger until it still has a little bite. Keep in the syrup in the fridge until needed.

Ingredients – cucumber spaghetti

2	cucumbers

Method

Cut cucumbers with the spaghetti attachment from the Benriner mandolin and cook for 10 seconds in seasoned boiling water and refresh in ice water. Drain and keep refrigerated.

Ingredients – marinated cucumber and lime juice

325g	of raw cucumber through the juicer, which produces:
250g	cucumber juice
75g	passed lime juice
30g	caster sugar
20g	grated ginger
5g	grated lime skin
2g	salt

Method

Infuse all the ingredients together for 1 hour.

Pass through a muslin cloth.

Ingredients – cucumber and lime jelly

300g	marinated cucumber and lime juice
3g	agar agar powder

Put a stainless steel container in the fridge and get all your ingredients ready before starting.

Method

Bring 100g of juice and the agar agar powder to the boil, quickly add remaining juice. Whisk thoroughly and set in a chilled. Leave to set for 2-3 hours and dice in neat squares. Reserve in refrigerator.

Ingredients – sour cream

100ml	of double cream
1	juice of a lime
	fine table salt
	ground white pepper

Method

In a stainless steel bowl whisk the double cream and the lime juice with fine table salt and ground white pepper until it reaches the

consistency of Greek yoghurt and keep in a squeezy bottle in the fridge.

To dress

Season the cucumber spaghetti with house dressing (see page 99) and a few snipped chives and place on the slates using a square mould. Brush the head and tail with olive oil and place at the top and bottom of the slate. With a long razor sharp slicer, thinly slice the lobster tails lengthways and place neatly on the spaghetti. Put the elbow and the claw, with the cartilage removed, next to it. Scatter some cucumber jelly dice on the tail and claws. Place pickled ginger squares, slightly smaller than a stamp, around. Squeeze sour cream then top with Sevruga caviar. Decorate with micro herbs, season lightly with Maldon sea salt and serve.

SCALLOPS STUFFED SKATE WING WITH BLOOD ORANGE MEUNIÉRE

Yield – 4 portions (or 8 as a starter)

"

This is one of our most attractive, vibrant and flavoursome dishes.

It's a seasonal dish to be made when blood oranges are in abundance.

The balance of flavours and dizzying colours make it a stand-out course.

"

Equipment

Tall jug blender
Deyhdrator (or oven at low temperature)
Sous vide machine

Ingredients – the skate

2x600g skate wing

Method

Order 600g skate wings from your fishmonger. They should be thick enough but not too big. You can easily do 4 portions with 1 wing.

With a sharp knife, starting from the top, slide it with slight angle along the cartilage and remove the flesh.

Keep it in the fridge. Work quickly because skate, like crab, has a reputation for developing an ammonia taste if left for too long.

Super gelatinous skate bones makes a very good fish stock so keep them wrapped in cling film in the freezer for another recipe.

Ingredients – the scallop mousse

150g   fresh scallop flesh

30g   egg white
150g   double cream

Method

In a tall blender, blitz the scallop flesh with the egg white, salt, pepper and cayenne. Add the cream little by little until homogenous.

Wrap some mousse in cling film and poach it to make sure it holds and the seasoning is right.

Reserve in a piping bag in the fridge.

Rolling the mousse and skate

Lay a double layer of cling film on a flat surface and season with salt.

Place one skate fillet on the cling film and pipe a layer of scallop mousse evenly (around 5mm thick) on the fish, and smooth with a spatula.

Roll the skate fillet onto itself and wrap the cling film around (like a swiss roll).

Roll tightly and close the end, securing with a piece of string.

Reserve in the fridge.

Ingredients – the butter

2x250g   high quality butter

Method

For this beurre noisette sauce, preparation is everything, so be military-like. Make sure all your equipment is ready before you start. You will need:

1 conical sieve
1 piece of damp muslin cloth
1 container full of ice cubes and a container to fit in it to stop the butter from browning

In a tall saucepan on a medium heat, melt the butter until it gets very brown, not black. As soon as it smells like hazelnuts, quickly pass it through the muslin cloth and the conical sieve. Refresh right away by putting the container in the iced water bath.
Put butter in fridge to set and once hard use, discarding any leftover milk at the bottom.

Ingredients – the croutons

3   slices of neatly diced white bread
150g   clarified butter

In a frying pan, on a moderate heat, fry the croutons in the clarified butter until golden. Place on top of a tray overlaid with absorbent paper. Season with salt as soon as they are out of the pan and keep in a dry place.

Ingredients – blood orange

3   blood oranges

Method

On a chopping board and with a sharp slicer, peel the blood oranges and segment them.

Cut them in half again. Keep them in some blood orange juice in the fridge until needed.

PARSLEY TUILLE

Method

Before chopping the parsley, pick out the best leaves. They should be quite big with at least 3 perfect leaves. Place them in a stainless steel bowl.

Drizzle with olive oil and salt and toss them gently.
Place over a cling filmed plate and put in a microwave at full blast for 4 minutes until completely crisp. If not crisp, repeat the operation for 2 minutes.

Once dried and translucent, reserve in the dehydrator until needed.

Chopped parsley

Using a knife, chop 15g of flat leaf parsley and keep it in a tureen in the fridge with a damp cloth on it.

Buttered baby gem

Trim the root of a baby gem and release the leaves. Blanch the green outer leaves, keeping the crunchy inner leaves for use in a different recipe.

Blanch in salted boiling water and refresh right away in ice water. Drain and keep in a dish between 2 j cloths in the fridge until needed.

SCALLOPS STUFFED SKATE WING WITH BLOOD ORANGE MEUNIERE continued

To assemble

Cook the fish in a water bath at 55c for 25 minutes.

A few minutes before serving, reheat the baby gem in a pan with a knob of butter.

Heat up the beurre noisette and when hot add a few capers and the blood orange segments.

Increase the sharpness with a trickle of lemon juice and season accordingly.

Serve in a warm bowl, adding the buttered baby gem to the bottom.

On a chopping board with a pair of scissors open the fish parcel. With a sharp serrated knife trim the end bit and gently cut in half. Place nicely on the side of the plate.

Add the chopped parsley to the butter sauce and pour it on the plate, placing the orange segments prettily. Scatter a few croutons on the top and then place the parsley crisps.

Serve at once.

CHECKERS
fish

SLOW POACHED JOHN DORY WITH VANILLA, CARROT PASTA AND LIME DRESSING

Yield – 3 portions (or 6 as a starter)

This is a dish I designed when still a young Chef de Partie at the Waterside Inn.

I created it after a trip to France.

It's a lovely spring dish, or salad, that takes osmosis to a new level.

Every ingredient leads to another and the surprisingly light, sweet and sour dressing is a great accompaniment for any poached fish.

Equipment

Vegetable juicer
Tall jug blender
Kenwood Major bowl
Pasta maker
Bamix hand blender
Benriner mandolin
Sous vide machine

Ingredients – the carrot reduction

In this recipe you will need some reduced carrot juice for the pasta and for the sauce, so make a large batch and divide accordingly.

4kg   of organic carrots, with their skin on

Method

Pass through a vegetable juicer. Put the juice in a large saucepan and reduce to 400g, stirring the bottom of the pan from time to time. Keep in the fridge in a container until needed. Any leftovers can be frozen.

Ingredients – the fish

John Dory is an unusual fish. It has a fillet on one side that divides itself naturally and one of those is big enough for a starter.

2   fillets of john dory
½   pod of a vanilla seed, with the seeds scraped onto the
           back of a small knife
3g   microplanned lime zest
20ml   chive oil (see page 83 for chive oil recipe)

Method

Divide the fillet into 3 natural fillets and evenly spread the vanilla seeds and fine lemon zest on each. Season with salt and pack 3 into a sous vide bag with 10ml of chive oil. Keep in the fridge.

110

THE CARROT PASTA

This unusual pasta works as well with reduced beetroot juice too.

It can be kept in the freezer if needs be.

Ingredients

60g	reduced carrot juice
2	yolks
1	whole eggs
250g	flour
6g	salt

Method

In a tall jug, and using a Braun 750w hand held blender, mix the eggs and flour until it becomes very smooth.

Pass through a fine mesh sieve and mix with the flour and salt in a Kenwood Major bowl with the paddle attachment.

Mix thoroughly at a low speed until homogenous.

Transfer to a stainless steel bowl and cover with cling film.

Rest in the fridge for at least 1 hour.

Make thin sheets in a pasta machine. Respect the resting time of 1-2 minutes every time.

Take it down a notch when the right thickness has been achieved (0.4) and let it dry for 7-9 minutes.

Cut the tagliatelle carefully with the tagliatelle cutter.

Store in the fridge between 2 layers of parchment in an air tight box with a lid on.

SLOW POACHED JOHN DORY WITH VANILLA, CARROT PASTA AND LIME DRESSING continued

Ingredients – sauce base

1	shallot roughly chopped
3	roughly sliced button mushrooms
100g	dry white wine
300g	fish stock
100g	freshly diced butter
150g	reduced carrot juice
35-50ml	lime juice
1	vanilla pod split in 2

Method

In a large saucepan, sweat the shallots and the mushrooms.

When slightly coloured, add the white wine and reduce until syrupy.

Add the fish stock and reduce by half. Pass this reduction thoroughly through a conical sieve into a clean saucepan and discard the vegetables.

Put the diced butter in the reduction and with a Bamix hand blender, blitz to a thick sauce. Add the reduced, warmed-up carrot juice to the base and emulsify again with the hand blender.

Add the lime juice and scrape the vanilla pod with the back of a small knife in the sauce. Emulsify and taste. Correct the seasoning.

Baby leeks and baby gem

Top and tail the baby leeks and trim the bottom of the baby gem salad. Cook them separately in seasoned simmering water until cooked.

Refresh them in iced water. Trim the outer leaves and keep in a container in the fridge.

TO DRESS

Dip the bag of fish in the sous vide machine at 55c for 30 minutes. Using a mandolin, slice 2 Chantenay carrots lengthways neatly and keep in salted iced water.

Heat the sauce gently in a saucepan and keep warm. It must not boil. Four minutes before the fish is cooked, lay the plates in front of you and heat the gems and leeks in warm fresh butter.

Pat dry and dress nicely on the plates. In a pasta basket, place a generous helping of pasta and dip it in seasoned boiling water with a good splash of olive oil.

Cook for 30 seconds and transfer to a warm stainless steel bowl with a dash of chive oil. Using a cooking fork and the palm of your hand, twist them into a nice oval shape and lay on the plate.

Pull the John Dory bag out of the water and place it on a wire rack with a tray under to collect the juice. With a sharp pair of scissors, open the bags and pull out the fish. Pat dry on a piece of paper towel and rest it on the seasoned baby gem.

Taste the sauce and correct the seasoning and the acidity accordingly.

Pour the sauce elegantly and finish with 2 slices of thinly-sliced Chantenay carrots and a dash of chive oil. Serve.

It is possible to simply steam or poach the Dory as opposed to using the sous vide and water-bath.

CHECKERS
fish

ATLANTIC LINE-CAUGHT TURBOT, SAFFRON AND THYME CRUST, GARLIC POMME MOUSSELINE AND SAUCE COTRIADE

Yield – 6 portions

This is a version of the famous Cotriade, or soupe de poisson a la Bretonne.

The dish can trace its roots to the Atlantic Coastline when the volume of the catch outstripped the demand. The excess stock would be used to make this delicious soup.

The depth of flavour is second to none and it's always better when it has matured for a couple of days.

You could substitute the turbot for scallop as a starter.

Equipment

Major Kenwood mixer (or similar)
Hand blender

Ingredients – the fish

Ask your fishmonger for 6 pieces of 180g, thick Atlantic turbot fillet, or, if you feel brave enough, buy a whole 2-3 kg turbot and prepare it yourself.

Ingredients – the crust

250g	soft butter
150g	finely grated extra Mature cheddar cheese
50g	finely grated parmesan cheese
75g	panko breadcrumbs
10g	thyme leaves
0.6g	saffron
5ml	Ricard

Method

In a mixer with the whisk attachment, whip up the butter until white and silky.

Change the whisk for a paddle and add both of the cheeses, Ricard, saffron and thyme leaves and beat for 1 minute.

Finally add the panko breadcrumbs and beat for 20 seconds.

When homogenous, roll the mixture thinly between 2 sheets of greaseproof paper and keep in the freezer until needed.

When you have determined the fish shape and size, cut the mixture down with a pair of scissors to match the fish's shape.

Keep in the freezer.

Ingredients – the cotriade

Don't be put off by the size of this recipe. It makes quite a lot of soup but it will be devoured by the gourmands in your household.

Cut the fish in large chunks so it does not disintegrate while roasting and also make sure to thoroughly remove the eyes and the gills.

2	medium gurnard cut into fat chunks
4	medium sea bream cut in 2
2	turbot heads and bones
2	large cod
4	roughly chopped up carrots
2	roughly chopped up leeks
2	roughly chopped large onions
6	chopped up ripe tomatoes
1	garlic head
1	large bouquet garni
1	bunch of parsley stalks
	dill stalks
30g	fennel seeds
30g	coriander seeds
400ml	white wine
250ml	Cognac
300ml	Ricard
100g	tomato purée
	fish stock to cover

Method

Lightly season with salt and swiftly pan fry the fish, getting a good colour.

Place in a very large pan alongside the tomatoes brandy, Ricard and tomato purée.

Colour the carrots, leeks, onions, celery and garlic and deglaze with the white wine. Reduce by half.

Bring the stockpot to the boil then gently simmer for 1 hour. Rest for 30 minutes.

Pass all of it through a mouli and then pass again through a conical sieve.

Reduce the soup to a sauce like consistency, making about 2 litres. You may not use it all but it will freeze really well.

ATLANTIC LINE-CAUGHT TURBOT, SAFFRON AND THYME CRUST, GARLIC POMME MOUSSELINE AND SAUCE COTRIADE continued

POMMES MOUSSELINE

At different times of the year, the best potato variety for mousseline changes.

Maris Piper and Desiree are great in summer but the best flavour comes from Red Washed in autumn.

We bake whole potatoes with the skin on instead of the traditional way of boiling them, we then add double cream and butter to balance flavour.

It tastes divine and is so versatile.

Lightly reheat just before service and in for this particular recipe we add just a touch of chopped garlic at the end.

Ingredients

4	large Red Washed potatoes, baked for 1 ½ hours at 180c
150 ml	of boiling double cream
50g	good quality butter

Method

When the potatoes are cooked, cut them in half and scoop the flesh into a mouli.

Pass the flesh through the mouli into a kitchen mixing bowl and beat at a very low speed with a paddle.

Add the cream little by little (don't over work).

To assemble

In a non-stick frying pan, heat some olive oil and roast the turbot, skin side down.

Heat the Cotriade in a skillet and keep at the ready.

Warm the mousseline and add a touch of crushed garlic to taste.

Put the roasted fish on a metal tray and lay the pre-cut crust on it, gently colour under the grill.

Pipe a generous amount of warm garlic mousseline into the middle of warmed plates.

Add a small piece of butter to the fish soup and aerate with a hand blender.

Check and correct the depth, consistency and seasoning.

Don't be afraid to add cayenne pepper as it is so much better with a kick.

Pour around the potato.

When the crust has melted on the turbot and become golden, place it on the mousseline and serve right away.

A side of buttered green beans or baby courgettes balances this rich dish beautifully.

CHECKERS
fish

DOVER SOLE PRINTANIÉRE

Yield – 6 portions

> This is a dish I designed when I was a young chef at the Waterside inn.
>
> I had to present it to my boss, Mr Roux, needless to say I was very nervous.
>
> It had to be absolutely right and when I eventually sent it to Michel Roux Snr's office, via Alain Roux, I hoped he would like it.
>
> When the plate came back, Alain lifted the argent cloche to reveal a completely empty plate. No further words were needed and I believe it is still on the menu to this very day.
>
> If you are serving the dish as a main course you can also serve some peeled new potatoes.

Equipment

Tall blending jug
Robot Coupe
Sous vide machine

Ingredients – the fish

12	large fillets of dover sole, bone free

Ingredients – the stuffing

300g	broad beans
100g	Dover sole flesh
8g	salt
30g	egg white
200g	double cream
	salt, pepper and cayenne pepper

Method

Make broad bean puree by shelling broad beans and blitzing in a tall narrow blender. Pass through a fine sieve. Blitz 100g of Dover sole flesh through a tall narrow blender and pass through a fine sieve.

Combine 90g of the blitzed Dover sole flesh with the salt and egg white in a scrupulously clean Robot Coupe bowl. Once homogenous add half of the broad bean puree while the Robot Coupe is running, using the pulse button setting. Add the double cream and season with salt, pepper and cayenne.

Reserve in a piping bag in the fridge.

Wrapping the sole

Lay a piece of cling film on a flat surface and sprinkle with some table salt. Place one sole fillet in the middle and pipe with 3 little lines of broad bean mousse around 0.5cm thick, and cover with another sole fillet.

Wrap cling film around tightly and repeat operation with all of the others. Keep in fridge until needed.

Ingredients – the sauce

10g	butter	100ml	cognac
100g	chopped shallots	300g	champagne
		300g	fish stock
100g	chopped white mushrooms	300g	double cream
		20g	fresh sorrel
300g	chopped lobster head	100g	parsley
		15g	lemon juice

Method

In a large pan, melt the butter and sweat the shallots and mushrooms. Add lobster heads and colour well. Deglaze with the cognac and reduce until syrupy.

Add champagne, fish stock, thyme and bay leaves and reduce by half.

Put in cream and reduce by half again, pass through a conical sieve, making sure to extract as much juice as possible. Add the remaining butter and pour the sauce into a tall narrow blender.

Add parsley and sorrel to the sauce and blitz until super-smooth. Pass through a conical sieve, correct the seasoning and add lemon juice according to taste.

Ingredients – the spring vegetables

Method

Allow 2 leeks per portion. Trim the top and bottom of the baby leek and peel away the first layer. Cook in salted simmering water. Refresh right away in ice water and reserve in a container in the fridge. For peas and broad beans, open the pod and shell the peas and cook them in salted water. Refresh in iced water. Prepare the broad beans in the same way as peas.

Cook the sole and serve

Cook the Dover sole in a water bath at 55c for 30 minutes. 2 minutes before the fish is cooked, warm up a serving dish in the oven and heat your vegetables in warm fresh butter. Heat up the sauce.

Take the fish out and cut the film around it. Trim the end with a sharp knife and slice it in 2. Place them delicately on the serving dish and put the vegetables on one side and the leek on top of the sole under a generous quenelle of caviar. Serve right away with the sauce in a sauce boat. Alternatively you could poach the sole without the mousse and still serve with the delicious sauce.

CHECKERS
fish

HOME SMOKED SCOTTISH SALMON, CARAMELISED ONION PURÉE, SAGE OIL DRESSING AND WINTER LEAVES

Yield – 6 portions

Salmon is very popular in our household

The flavours are heavenly together, with the meatiness of the home smoked salmon dovetailing perfectly with the classic onion and stage sage combination.

We use Loch Duart Scottish salmon, though wild salmon is best if you can get a consistent supply.

Equipment

1 smoker (or an old tray layered with foil, a closely-fitting lid and a rack that fits inside and is propped up by 4 balls of scrunched up foil)
300g oak chips
Dehydrator (or oven at low temperature)

Ingredients – the salmon

Ask your fish supplier for a thick piece of fillet from the middle of the fish, weighing approximately 1kg.

On a flat surface, place the salmon skin side up and run a knife over the skin to scrape off any scales that may have been left on it.

Now turn the fillet around and with the tip of your finger graze the top of the flesh to make sure there are no pin bones left in it.

If you find any, remove them with tweezers. Wrap the salmon in cling film and put it in the freezer, skin side down, on a flat tray for 3 hours.

When semi-frozen, lay the salmon on a chopping board and neatly score the skin with a sharp slicing knife.

Trim the belly and the top of the fillet for a slick cut. You want all of the pieces to be the same shape.

Now divide the salmon into 6 fillets and rub with sea salt. Leave it in for 8 minutes. Rinse thoroughly and reserve on the wire rack of a smoker.

Heat up the oak chips in your smoker. When a strong smoke is achieved turn off the heat and smoke your salmon fillets for 2 minutes each. If the smoke is too light, smoke for a minute or two longer.

CHECKERS
fish

HOME SMOKED SCOTTISH SALMON, CARAMELISED ONION PURÉE, SAGE OIL DRESSING AND WINTER LEAVES continued

Ingredients – the onion purée

2	large peeled onions
250g	butter
100ml	double cream

Method

With a sharp mandolin, slice the onions very thinly and cook in a large pan with the melted butter on a very gentle heat. Cook until light brown but not burned.

That should take about 1-and-a-half to 2 hours. Drain the onions in a colander and discard the butter.

Add the double cream to the pan and transfer the onions back in.

Bring to the boil. Pass the mixture in a tall blender and blitz until very smooth.

When ready pass through a fine mesh conical sieve and correct the seasoning. Keep in the fridge until needed.

Equipment

Conical sieve
Kitchen cheminee
Muslin cloth
2 kitchen bowls
500g ice cubes
Food blender
Hand held thermometer

Ingredients – sage oil

30g	of roughly chopped sage
250ml	olive oil
	salt

Method

In the pan and over a stove, use the hand held thermometer to bring the oil to 60c.

Put the sage into the blender and add the hot oil whist the blender is running.

Add a pinch of salt and leave it on for a minute.

Immediately pass through a conical sieve lined with a muslin cloth over a bowl over ice (this prevents the oil discolouring). Once cold, store in a squeezy bottle in the fridge until required.

Ingredients – the sage dressing

100ml	sage oil
30ml	lemon juice
	salt pepper

Method

Mix all the above ingredients using a hand blender and correct the seasoning and acidity to suit your preference.

Store in a squeezy bottle and it's ready to go.

To dress

Warm up the onion puree and decant it into a squeezy bottle. Keep the sage dressing handy.

Gently heat a non-stick frying pan and drizzle some olive oil into it.

Place the salmon skin side down and cook for 1-and-a-half minutes until the skin gets crispy.

Cut off the gas and turn the salmon around, leaving the residual heat of the pan to carry on cooking the fish.

Rest on a disposable towel, which will absorb any un-wanted fat.

On a warm plate squeeze a substantial amount of onion purée and swoosh it with the back of a cooking spoon.

Place the cooked salmon on top and with a drizzle of sage oil. Dress the plate with a few salad leaves coated in the sage dressing.

Arrange neatly on the plate.

Scatter a few crispy sage leaves onto the dish and serve at once.

THE SAGE LEAVES

Method

Pick out the best-looking leaves from a bunch and roll them in a bowl with salt and olive oil.

Set the rest aside for use in the sage oil.

Cling film a plate and arrange the leaves nicely on it.

Put more cling film over them and cook for 4 minutes in a microwave. Check for crispiness and if slightly soggy, cook for a further 1-2 minutes until crisp.

Once crisp, reserve in the dehydrator or an airtight container.

POACHED OCTOPUS, SWEET AND SOUR RED PEPPER COULIS, SQUID INK PASTA

Yield – 6 portions

> Guests are often very surprised to like octopus.
>
> It has a reputation for being chewy and the appearance can be a little off putting.
>
> However, correctly prepared octopus can have truly superb tenderness and flavour.
>
> This dish is great served as a canapé but even better as a starter.
>
> It is accompanied by a delicious sweet and sour red pepper coulis and the black squid ink pasta offers contrasting texture, colour and taste.

Equipment
Sous vide machine
Combi oven
Tall jug blender
Kenwood Major mixer (or similar)

Ingredients – the octopus

1	large octopus
	sea salt

Method

Cut the head off, remove and discard the beak.

Wash thoroughly and cover in sea salt for 2 minutes.

Rinse well and place in a sous vide machine with a bit of olive oil.

Ensure the suckers are well tucked in because they tend to overcook.

The tentacles cook alongside the body at 58c for 3 hours. They are not mixed with the body because they can stain it.

Cook the body in a combi oven for 10 hours at 83c at full steam.

When tentacles are cooked, refresh the bag in iced water.

When cold open the bag and pat the tentacles dry.

Trim the top and with a sharp knife. Divide neatly in 6, keeping their shape and the suckers on.

Lay on a new j cloth. Reserve in the fridge.

When dried, sous vide again and reserve the bag in the fridge.

You will reheat later.

POACHED OCTOPUS, SWEET AND SOUR RED PEPPER COULIS, SQUID INK PASTA continued

Ingredients – the red peppers

5	red peppers
	olive oil
	salt
	pepper
	cayenne
	balsamic vinegar
	caster sugar

Method

In an olive-oiled baking tray, season and roast 6 red peppers at 180c.

Turn them over every 10 minutes, cooking for around 75 minutes so that they are cooked but have a bite.

Peel and deseed them.

Keep 6 nice sides to use later on and weigh what's left.

Put all the pepper flesh in a tall blender and add 10 percent of the weight of boiled balsamic vinegar boiled with 10 percent of caster sugar.

Incorporate while the machine is running and blitz for 2 minutes until very smooth, pass through a conical sieve, store in a plastic container with lid in the fridge.

Ingredients – Black ink pasta

This recipe will yield more than the quantity required, so freeze the remained (unrolled) for future use.

250g	double 00 Italian flour
2	whole eggs
3	egg yolks
7g	salt
15g	black squid ink

Method

Weigh all of the ingredients.

Place the flour and salt in the Kenwood Major bowl with the paddle.

Put the squid ink, eggs and egg yolks in a tall container and blitz with a hand blender until very smooth.

Incorporate the squid ink mix with the flour and salt and mix for 5 minutes in the Kenwood at a low speed until homogenous.

If a bit dry, add a little water (5cl). Take the dough out and roll into a ball. Wrap in cling film and leave to rest in the fridge for 1 hour.

Using a pasta machine, roll down the dough gradually until it gets really thin (0.3). Make sure you rest the sheets between each turn.

Cut some circles with a fluted 7cm cutter and loosely wrap in cling film.

Using a lightly dampened paint brush, dot the middle of the pasta circles. Turn it over.

Place your index finger in the middle of the pasta to use as a stabiliser and with your thumb and finger, squeeze, though not too tight or it will be too dense to cook evenly.

The fluted discs should be pinched into a bow.

Repeat the operation with them all and air dry for 2 hours on a tray lined with a lightly floured baking parchment sheet. When they are holding their shape and dry, place between 2 paper towels and keep in the fridge.

TO ASSEMBLE

Place the cast iron griddle pan on the gas and leave it on until its really hot.

Put a large pan of salted water with a squeeze of olive oil on the hob, to cook the pasta.

Set the sous vide at 80c and when the temperature is reached dip the octopus bag in for 10 minutes.

Smudge the peppers in olive oil and season with salt.

Turn off the flames under the griddle and place on the grill, designing a nice criss cross pattern.

When done, transfer to a plate and keep warm.

Warm up the red pepper coulis in a small sauce pan and transfer it to a squeezy bottle.

Lay 6 warm bowls in front of you and squeeze some hot, sweet and sour pepper coulis at the bottom of the plates.

Place the warm griddled pepper in the centre, followed by a few baby spinach leaves dressed with house dressing (page 99).

Open the octopus bag with a pair of sharp scissors and tip gently on a tray layed with paper towels.

Pat dry and place attractively on the plate.

Dip the pasta bows in the boiling water for 45-60 seconds and remove with a slotted spoon and reserve onto an oiled stainless steel tray.

Place the elements elegantly on the plates and serve immediately.

CHECKERS
fish

STUFFED SQUID ANTIBOISE

Yield – 6 portions

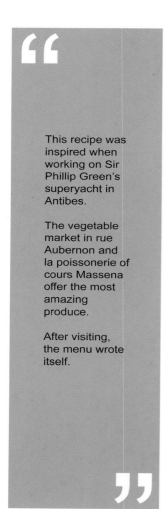

"

This recipe was inspired when working on Sir Phillip Green's superyacht in Antibes.

The vegetable market in rue Aubernon and la poissonerie of cours Massena offer the most amazing produce.

After visiting, the menu wrote itself.

"

Equipment

Sous vide machine

Ingredients – the squid

6   x400g whole squid

Method

Pull out the tentacles, remove and discard the beak.

Cut in 2, with 4 tentacles on each side.

Wash thoroughly and sous vide (the tentacles).

Dig your finger in the body and clean under running water, making sure all the guts are removed.

Take out the spine, which looks translucent, like clear plastic.

Wash meticulously again under running water.

Remove the wings and peel the skin like a sock.

Wash again.

Season and place in a sous vide bag and cook in the water bath for 3 hours at 59c, refreshing the bag right away in ice water.

Ingredients – the stuffing

100g   chopped spinach, sautéed in fresh butter with a clove of garlic at the end of a fork
35g   finely grated Parmesan
25g   diced fried chorizo, adding the oil to the mix
20g   toasted breadcrumbs salt, pepper, cayenne

Method

Mix all ingredients in a stainless steel bowl and season well.

Reserve in a piping bag.

Stuffing the squid

When the bodies of the cooked squid are cold take them out of the bag and pat dry them.

With a disposable tea towel, dry all the interior.

Using the piping bag full of stuffing, very delicately fill the squid but do not overfill or they will split while roasting.

Close with a toothpick.

Reserve in the fridge.

Ingredients – la sauce Antiboise

2	finely chopped banana shallots
1	garlic clove crushed, reduced to a fine paste
6	peeled, deseeded and neatly diced super ripe tomatoes on the vine
100g	concasse de tomates (recipe below)
15	pitted black olives cut in half
15	pitted green olives cut in half
10cl	lemon juice
10cl	of extra virgin olive oil
15	leaves of basil cut in fine ribbons

Method

Gently heat the concasse of tomatoes and add the shallots, garlic, diced tomato, olive oil and warm it through. Add all the remaining ingredients and season just before serving.

Ingredients – concasse de tomates (fondue de tomates)

1	dash of olive oil
1	finely chopped banana shallot
1	crushed and chopped head of garlic
1	dessert spoon of tomato paste
5	tomatoes, boiled for 20 seconds, refreshed peeled, quartered, deseeded and roughly diced (8mm)
1	bouquet garni

Method

Sweat the shallots in the olive oil until translucent. Add the crushed garlic and sweat for another 2 minutes. Add the tomato dice, the paste and bouquet garni and cook gently until almost dry. Season accordingly and reserve in the fridge until needed.

Cook and dress

Turn the oven to 180c full fan and heat an oven-friendly, non-stick frying pan. In olive oil, colour the stuffed squid on 4 sides and bake for 2 minutes on each flank. While the fish is cooking warm up the Antiboise sauce and quickly pan fry the tentacles.

Work quickly and dress the sauce and tentacles nicely on the side of the warm plate. When the squid is ready insert a long spike to ensure it is warm in the middle. Slice them equally in 3 and dress attractively on the plate. Brush the tops with olive oil and decorate with a few micro-basil leaves and serve right away.

ASSIETTE OF PIGLET BEST END, CRISPY-TENDER BELLY, BOUDIN NOIR, CARAMELISED PEAR, POMMES MOUSSELINE MADEIRA JUS

Yield – 4 portions

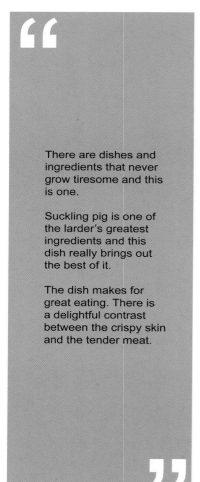

There are dishes and ingredients that never grow tiresome and this is one.

Suckling pig is one of the larder's greatest ingredients and this dish really brings out the best of it.

The dish makes for great eating. There is a delightful contrast between the crispy skin and the tender meat.

Equipment

Braun hand blender
Stainless steel perforated gastronorm tray
Blast chiller
Tall blender jug
Combi oven

Ingredients – the meat

2   best ends of piglet

With the tip of a sharp butcher's knife, score the skin of the rack and salt it for 30 minutes.

Rinse well and keep it in the fridge until needed.

1   belly

Remove all the bones and sprinkle some sea salt all over it. Leave the salt to soften the flesh and season the meat for around an hour.

Rinse thoroughly and bake in duck fat for 3-4 hours at 90c.

Once cooked, the meat will be very, very soft. Leave it to cool in the fat until tepid.

Wrap the belly in cling film and press it between 2 flat trays in the fridge until the next day.

When completely cold, unwrap it and trim the fat on the outside.

Cut it with a sharp knife through the middle and score it precisely and gently.

Keep on a tray in the fridge.

ASSIETTE OF PIGLET BEST END, CRISPY-TENDER BELLY, BOUDIN NOIR, CARAMELISED PEAR, POMMES MOUSSELINE MADEIRA JUS continued

The boudin noir

We made our boudin noir (black pudding) at the Herbert Arms and have also made it at The Checkers since our first day. It's a staple for us.

When the blood arrives tip a cap of red wine vinegar into it to prevent it from clotting. Make sure you pass the blood used through a conical sieve.

Ingredients

3metres	fat sausage skin (available from a good butcher)
20g	butter
400g	chopped onions
20g	chopped garlic, with green stem removed
250g	peeled cored and diced Bramley apple
500g	diced pork fat, wth the skin removed
150ml	double cream
100ml	full fat milk
450ml	red wine
30g	salt
6g	ground black pepper corn
30g	breadcrumbs
2g	four spices (ground pepper, cloves, nutmeg and ginger)
1l	pig's blood

Method

The first job is to ensure you have enough good quality sausage skin.

Run some water through the skin to make sure there are no holes. In a large pan, confit the onions and garlic with the butter.

Cook them very slowly so that they do not take on any colour. It should take around 30 minutes.

Add the apple and cook for a further 30 minutes. In a boiling pan of water, cook the pork fat for 2 minutes, boiling all the time.

Drain and add it to the mixture. Cook for a further 40 minutes. Now add the cream, milk, wine, breadcrumbs, spice, salt and pepper and cook for 20 minutes.

Using a hand blender with the metal head propeller attached, blitz the mixture until it is very fluid.

Off the heat, add the passed blood and incorporate thoroughly with the blender. Place back on the heat and cook gently until you reach 55c. Stir all the time with a heat resistant spatula making sure to scrape the bottom of the pan from time to time.

Using a funnel and measuring jug, tip the blood mixture into the sausage skin and knot 3 by 3. It should not be too tight and it should not be too loose.

Lay the freshly filled boudin into a stainless steel perforated gastronorm tray and cook in a combi oven at full steam with maximum fan for:
85c for 10min
83c for 15min
81c for 20min

When cooked, cool in the blast chiller and keep in the fridge.

This makes a large quantity of boudin noir, it is great for breakfast or alternatively cut down the quantities accordingly.

Ingredients – the pears

10	peeled Comice pears
1l	water
250g	caster sugar
Juice	of 3 lemons
1	stick of cinnamon
3	crushed star anise

Method

Bring the water, spices and sugar to the boil and dip in the peeled pear. Cover with baking parchment (a cartouche) and simmer for 5-10 minutes until cooked but not mushed. Cool in the liquid.

Slice the 4 pears in 2 and with a melon baller scoop the pips out leaving a nice neat hole. Place them face down in a non-stick frying pan with a little oil and bake for 30-45 minutes at 180c until they are nicely caramelised. When they are ready, turn them out and keep them warm.

Ingredients – the pear purée

500g	pear flesh (from poached pears)
125g	pear juice (liquor from poached pears)
7g	agar agar powder

Method

Bring the juice and the agar agar to the boil, whisking continuously. When boiling, pour over the pear flesh in a tall blender jug and blitz for 2 minutes.

Pour the purée onto a stainless steel tray and leave to set in the fridge for 1 hour. Once set, put the purée in the tall jug blender again and run it for 2 minutes.

When velvety and silky, pass through a fine mesh conical sieve and reserve in the fridge.

For Pommes Mousseline, see page 117

Ingredients – the Madeira jus

1kg	chopped piglet bones
1	roughly chopped onion
250ml	white wine
800ml	pork stock
800ml	veal stock
750ml	sweet madeira
	salt, pepper, caster sugar
1	garlic head
1	sprig of thyme

Method

Put a splash of oil in a large deep pan and caramelise the bones. Add the onions and colour them a little more. Deglaze with the white wine and reduce it until it's syrupy. Add both of the stocks and bring to the boil.

Simmer for an hour and pass through a conical sieve, then twice through a muslin cloth. Reduce at full boil until the consistency is thick but light. At the same time reduce the 685g of madeira in a pan on its own until it is very syrupy. Add that to the reduced sauce.

Finish the sauce with a splash of Madeira, salt and pepper and add some sugar to taste and a knob of butter to emulsify.

DRESS AND SERVE

Heat up a heavy bottom, oven-friendly frying pan. Squeeze some vegetable oil in the pan until it gets really hot and place the rack of piglet skin side down and create the crackling. When the skin is golden and bubbly bake at 190c until the core reach 70c. It should take 25-30 minutes. Rest for 10-15 minutes.

Place the confit piglet belly skin-side down in a frying pan, without oil, and bake at 190c for 10 minutes. When hot, tender and with a crispy skin, turn it over on a tray next to the rack. Peel the boudin noir and bake in an oven-friendly tray with some olive oil for 3 minutes on each side and keep alongside the rack and the belly.

Warm up the sauce and sweat some spinach and garlic. Season with salt, pepper and nutmeg.

Warm the mousseline and plate in a teardrop shape on a warm plate. Quenelle a nice measure of warm pear purée and place the spinach at the end of the plate. Lay the caramelised pear on the top.

With a serrated knife, slice the rack in an attractive shape and place in the middle of the plate with hot pork belly next to it. Trim the end and slice the boudin noir in 2. Place that on the plate.

Finally, taste the sauce and correct if necessary. Pour and serve.

CORN-FED CHICKEN TOURTE
FAÇON OREILLER
DE LA BELLE AURORE
Yield – 4 portions

This is a very old French dish that dates back around 400 years.

It was first put together by Brillat Savarin and was called beautiful Aurore's pillow.

It has survived the test of time because it's so good: a classic example of a classic. You could substitute the chicken for partridge or guinea fowl.

However, it's a difficult recipe to get right.

To maximise your chances of success make sure you are very organised and use the best quality all-butter puff pastry.

Butcher the chicken

On a chopping board, with a sharp knife, delicately take off the breasts. Remove and discard the skin. Pull out the fillet under the breast and remove the sinew.

Reserve the breasts in the fridge and roughly dice the fillets. Keep in a stainless steel bowl in the fridge. Detach the chicken leg and cut them neatly in 2 on the joint. Bone out the femur bone, trim the sinew and remove any unwanted fat. Peel the skin and dice the flesh. Mix in the bowl with the diced fillets.

Chop up carcass, wings and drumsticks into 1cm pieces for sauce.

Ingredients – the farce

100g	diced chicken flesh (legs and fillet)
50g	diced pork fat
1	generous dash of cognac
1	generous dash of sweet Madeira
50g	double cream
10g	chopped tarragon
10g	snipped chives
	fine salt, ground white pepper and cayenne to taste

Method

Marinate the chicken and fat in the cognac and Madeira for 24 hours. Pass the meat and alcohol through a meat grinder and beat the cream and herbs into it using a maryse. Season with salt, pepper and cayenne. Fry a little test piece to ensure the seasoning and texture are up to the highest standard. When satisfied, spread the farce between 2 sheets of cling film and spread at 1cm. Cover and store in the fridge.

Ingredients – the foie gras

In a hot pan, sear two frozen 25g slices of foie gras (this is to colour them only) and keep alongside the chicken breasts.

Ingredients – the pancakes

250ml	milk
2	eggs
65g	flour
5g	finely chopped chives
5g	finely diced tarragon
	fine salt and ground white pepper to taste

Method

In a stainless steel bowl, use a hand blender to combine the eggs and milk. Sift in the flour and whisk until homogenous.

Pass the mix through a fine mesh conical sieve and add the herbs. Season to taste and rest for an hour.

Cook gently in a non-stick frying pan and keep in the fridge until needed.

THE SAUCE
Ingredients

250g	chopped bones from the chicken
2	roughly chopped carrots
2	roughly chopped shallots
1	roughly chopped stick of celery
250ml	white wine
1.5l	chicken stock
1l	veal stock
	salt and pepper
10	chopped garlic cloves and a sprig of thyme

Method

In a deep pan, roast all the bones with a dash of vegetable oil until golden. Add the vegetables and cook for a further 2 minutes. Deglaze the pan with the white wine and reduce until syrupy. Add the stocks and cook for 1 hour. Pass through a conical sieve then through a muslin cloth. Reduce the sauce to a single-cream-like consistency and infuse with the chopped garlic cloves and thyme for 10 minutes. Correct the seasoning and pass through a conical sieve.

136

CORN-FED CHICKEN TOURTE FAÇON OREILLER DE LA BELLE AURORE continued

Ingredients – the carrots

200g	Chantenay carrots
500ml	water
75g	sugar
100g	butter
	thyme and bay leaves
	generous pinch of salt

Method

Bring the peeled, Chantenay carrots to the boil in a syrup made from the other ingredients.

Cook at a simmer for 5-10 minutes and leave to cool in the liquor.

When cold, cut them in 2 lengthways.

Ingredients – greens

1	savoy cabbage

Trim the outer leaves of a savoy cabbage and pick out the best looking ones.

Blanch them in salted boiling water until tender, which should take 1-2 minutes.

Refresh them in ice water right away. Drain and keep between 2 clean kitchen towels until needed.

ASSEMBLING THE DISH

On a piece of baking parchment, roll the puff pastry to a 3mm thickness and keep in the fridge.

On a piece of cling film, place the farce (slightly bigger than the chicken breasts) and lay the seasoned chicken breast on it.

Place another layer of farce on top of the chicken and place the seared foie gras on top. Finally top up with the remaining layer of farce. Roll gently in the film and wait for 2 hours. When cold, unwrap the farce-chicken-foie gras meat loaf and tightly wrap the blanched leaves of cabbage around. Repeat the operation with the pancakes then return to the fridge until cold.

Paint some egg wash on the puff pastry and lay the chicken farce parcel on it and the foie gras facing down.

Use the 4 corners of the chicken farce as marks to cut an open envelope-like shape then close it neatly on the chicken farce. Roll it onto a non-stick oven tray and store in the fridge.

For the egg wash: in a stainless steel bowl, beat 1 whole egg, 1 egg yolk and a dash of milk with a whisk.

Add a pinch of salt and sugar and pass through a conical sieve.

With a pastry brush, egg wash the puff pastry 3 times with 5 minute intervals each time, storing in the fridge. If you are going to present it on the table, decorate with the tip of a knife.

Cook at 180c for 1 hour: the middle of the loaf must reach 63c. When cooked transfer to a wire rack and rest for 10 minutes.

While the pie is resting, heat a non-stick frying pan and roast the carrot with half olive oil and half butter to a golden colour and keep warm.

Warm the pre-cooked cabbage in melted fresh butter and heat the sauce. Plate up the warm vegetables, cut a thick slice and serve with pomme mousseline (see page 117) and white wine jus.

ROASTED CROWN OF PIGEON DE BRESSE, CUISSES CONFITES, RED ONIONS AND SULTANAS, COUS COUS, DATE BUBBLES, FOIE GRAS, ORANGE GASTRIQUE REDUCTION

Yield – 4 portions

This sophisticated dish allies modern and classic brilliantly.

It is a new modern classic.

Contemporary techniques are used to enhance a model combination.

It is a real winner.

Equipment
Combi oven
Tall jug blender

Ingredients – the pigeons

4	pigeons

Butchery

With a pair of sharp scissors cut out the crown, leaving the legs and the lungs still attached. With a sharp knife, scrape the wishbone. Keep the crown in the fridge.

Using a boning knife, detach the legs from the carcass and dip them in salt for 25 minutes. Chop all the bones for the sauce.
Wash the salted legs thoroughly.

Ingredients – foie gras

4x75g	slices special frying rougie foie gras, cut in 3

Ingredients – sauce

All	the bones from the pigeons carcass diced in 1cm x 1cm pieces (300g-400g)
1	peeled and roughly diced carrot
2	peeled and roughly diced small shallots
50ml	red wine
300g	veal stock

300ml	chicken stock (or pigeon stock)
5g	orange peel

Ingredients – gastrique

55g	caster sugar
100ml	orange juice
50ml	red wine vinegar

Method

In a large pan, colour the bones with a bit of olive oil and add the vegetables. Colour a little more. Deglaze with the wine and reduce until syrupy. Add the stocks and the orange peel and simmer for 90 minutes.

In a different pan make the gastrique by caramelising the sugar until golden brown and deglazing with the vinegar. Reduce until syrupy, add the orange juice and again reduce until syrupy. Add to sauce. When the 90 minutes are up, pass the sauce in a container through a fine mesh conical sieve.

Pass again through a double lined muslin cloth over a large saucepan. Reduce to consistency similar to single cream.

Correct the seasoning with fine table salt and the acidity with fresh orange juice or, if it is too tart, add a pinch of sugar. Refrigerate.

ROASTED CROWN OF PIGEON DE BRESSE, CUISSES CONFITES, RED ONIONS AND SULTANAS, COUS COUS, DATE BUBBLES, FOIE GRAS, ORANGE GASTRIQUE REDUCTION

Ingredients – cooking the legs

800ml	goose fat
1	garlic head
1	sprig of thyme
1	bay leaf

The salted pigeon legs

Method

In a medium oven-friendly saucepan, melt the goose fat on the hob.

Add the garlic, thyme and bay leaf and submerge the legs.

Carefully cut a cartouche (circle of parchment) and cover the top of the pan and bake at 90c in a combi oven for 240 minutes.

When ready, pull a leg out with a fork and the meat should come off the bone easily. If not, return to the oven for an additional hour. When ready, leave to cool in the fat.

Ingredients – candied oranges skin

2	large oranges
100g	sugar
50g	glucose
50-150g	water

Method

Peel 2 large oranges and trim the pith.

Using a chopping knife, julienne the peel and put in a

pan with cold water. Bring the pan to the boil. When boiling drain the pan and refill with cold water and repeat the process 3 times.

When done, place in a pan with the sugar, glucose and water and cook at a very low heat for 120-180 minutes.

Add a little water from time to time, until very soft.

Transfer to a container in the fridge.

Oranges segments

Cut the top and bottom of the oranges and peel using a knife. Take care not to leave too much flesh on the pith.

Segment the oranges and cut each segment in half. Before discarding, squeeze the centre of the orange over the segments to obtain all the juice.

Reserve in the fridge.

The dates bubbles (reverse spherification)

Ingredients – dates puree

200g	medjool dates
	water to cover

Method

In a large saucepan, bring the dates and water to the boil and simmer for 5 minutes. Leave to cool in the pan. Blitz the cooked dates and the liquid through a tall jug blender. Liquidise and pass through a fine mesh conical sieve. If too stiff add a bit of water.

Ingredients – liquid centre date bubbles

50g	water
40g	sugar
450g	passed date puree
15g	calcium lactate
3g	xantham gum
10g	caster sugar

Method

In a saucepan, boil the sugar and water to make a stock syrup. As soon as it's boiling, take it off the heat and leave to cool.

Mix the calcium lactate, xanthan gum and caster sugar in a bowl. In a fresh saucepan, mix the syrup, date puree and calcium lactate, xanthan gum and sugar mix.

Bring all to the boil, whisking all the time. Pass through a fine mesh conical sieve and cool at room temperature.

We freeze the puree in round silicon moulds (3cm diameter).

Ingredients – the alginate bath

50g	sugar
8g	sodium alginate
1l	water

Method

Place the water in a saucepan and place it on the hob over low heat.

Mix together the sugar and sodium alginate and add it to the water and whisk continuously until dissolved.

Bring it to 75c. Take off the heat immediately and strain into a deep container and cool.

Method – Making the bubbles

Take the silicon mat out of the freezer and pop the frozen domes out of their moulds.

Submerge them in the alginate bath and leave them there for 10 minutes.

They must not touch each other.

With a slotted spoon, move them a little in the bath or they will stick to the bottom.

When ready, remove the bubbles with a slotted spoon and place them in a bowl of warm water in order to remove any excess of alginate mixture.

Stock the bubbles in a container of water in the fridge.

Ingredients – the couscous

500g	fine couscous
500g	freshly squeezed orange juice
60cl	olive oil
2	finely chopped and sweated red onions
50g	sultanas soaked in strong tea for 24h and drained
50g	whole roasted pine nuts
40g	candied orange peel

Method

Bring the orange juice to the boil and pour it over the semolina in a stainless steel bowl. Add the olive oil and cover with cling film. Leave to cook for 15 minutes. Using a fork, toss up the semolina until it becomes airy and fluffy. When ready, add all the remaining ingredients and season accordingly.

To assemble

Add a dash of olive oil to a frying pan and place over a high heat. Colour the pigeon's skin until golden brown and place the crown on a Gastronorm plain oven tray.

Make a beurre noisette with 200g of salted butter and add 3 garlic cloves cut in 2 and a sprigs of thyme

Pour it over the breasts. Cook in a combi oven set on mixed heat with 5% humidity at 60c until the core of the breasts reach 57c. Check frequently.

While the pigeon cooks, heat a pan of water to about 60c and transfer to a tall container. Drop the date bubbles in for 4-5 minutes. In a saucepan, heat the orange segments in the orange juice.

Warm up a non-stick frying pan and colour the pigeon legs, skin side down, until crispy and golden, but just hot in the middle. With a pair of sharp scissors cut the knee bone and trim the meat around the top of the leg to get a professional finish.

Remove the thigh bone and keep warm, skin side up. Heat up a non-stick frying pan and season the 12 pieces of foie gras. Cook until just done.

Take off the heat and place on a tray next to the crispy legs. Heat the cous cous in a saucepan and gently warm up the sauce. With a slotted spoon, fish out the bubbles and drain on a paper towel. Do the same with the warm orange segments.

Lay the warm plate in front of you and taste and dress the bubbles, foie gras, couscous and legs elegantly.

At the last minute use a boning knife to take the breasts off the bones and trim any excess bits. Arrange nicely on top of the warm couscous. Taste and pour the sauce over. Serve at once.

ROASTED GUINEA FOWL BREAST, STUFFED LEG, TRANCHE DE FOIE GRAS, BOUDIN BLANC, MONBAZILLAC SAUCE

Yield – 4-6 portions

This is a beautiful and rich dish that celebrates the perfect harmony between this underrated gamey bird and one of France's most beautiful vineyards.

It is a special dish for a special occasion and reminds me of my Auntie Evelyne Gouyou, one of the best household cuisiniere I know.

She lives in Bouniagues, only a few kilometres from Monbazillac.

Equipment

Sous vide machine
Kenwood Major food processor (or similar)
Tall jug blender
Combi oven
Blast chiller
Blender

Ingredients – the guinea fowl

2   guinea fowl

Method

Butchery: With a sharp boning knife, take off the legs, but leave the oysters on. Cut neatly between the leg muscle and drumstick.

Debone the leg muscle, keeping the bones for the sauce, and trim the sinew and fat on the flesh side. Place the trimmed leg between 2 pieces of cling film and bat them down with a kitchen hammer to a 1cm high square. Reserve in fridge.

Debone the drum stick and dice the flesh aside for the farce. With a pair of sharp scissors cut out the crown. Cut again under the breasts so you only have the 2 breasts and the bone attached to them. Place the breast crown in coarse sea salt for 25 minutes and rinse well, then sous vide the crown with a generous spoonful of duck fat and pre-cook in

the water bath at 55c for 90 minutes. Refresh the bag in ice water and when cold open the bag and reserve crown in the fridge, ready to roast.

Ingredients – the farce

To stuff 4 legs you will need:

200g	guinea fowl flesh	
100g	pork fat	
100g	double cream	
	a generous spoonful of Cognac	
	a generous spoonful of Madeira	
10g	chopped tarragon	
10g	chopped up flat parsley	
	salt and cayenne pepper	

Method

In a kitchen bowl, marinate the guinea fowl flesh, pork fat and alcohol for 24 hours, then pass through a kitchen grinder attachment on the Kenwood Major into the Kenwood's bowl. Add the salt, cayenne, herbs and set in the machine with the paddle on.

Start mixing very gently and pour in the cream little by little until completely homogenous. Fry a little bit of the farce in a skillet to check for seasoning and texture. Correct if necessary. Reserve in a disposable piping bag in the fridge.

143

ROASTED GUINEA FOWL BREAST, STUFFED LEG, TRANCHE DE FOIE GRAS, BOUDIN BLANC, MONBAZILLAC SAUCE continued

To stuff the leg

Lay a double piece of cling film on a worktop. Squeeze a bit of olive oil and sprinkle some fine salt on top. Place the battered leg, skin down, and pipe some stuffing on the top. It should be just enough to comfortably close the leg and roll the cling film tightly around it.

Repeat with all the legs. When all rolled, cook sous vide at 65c for 3 hours. Refresh in ice water and unwrap with a pair of scissors. Pat dry and keep in the fridge.

Ingredients – boudin blanc

50g	fine white breadcrumbs
65ml	milk
1	finely diced banana shallot
20g	diced fresh butter
100g	roughly diced guinea flesh
100g	diced pork fat, no skin
3	whole eggs
250ml	double cream
40ml	white port
10g	cornflour
10g	salt
50g	roughly chopped pistachios
25g	brioche crumbs

Method

Boil the milk and add the breadcrumbs. Take off the heat and leave to rest for 30 minutes. Sweat the shallots in the butter and reserve on the side.

In a tall blender, blitz the flesh fat and egg until very smooth and while the machine is running add the milk and bread paste (panade).

When homogenous, transfer to a stainless steel bowl and with a maryse, carefully fold in the double cream but do not over-beat.

Then add the shallots, cornflour, white port, salt, pistachios and finally the brioche crumbs. Reserve in a piping bag.

Carefully push the filling in the sausage skin. Divide the boudin with a piece of string, the size of your finger. Punch a few tiny holes in them with a sewing needle and lay on a stainless steel perforated gastronorm tray.

Cook in a combi oven at full steam:
    87c for 9mn
    83c for 4mn
    81c for 5mn
When cooked, transfer in a plastic box to the blast chiller. When cold, peel and reserve in the fridge.

Ingredients – the lentils (see page 103)

Ingredients – the carrots

Theses are not your average carrot wheels. They are cut thick at 1.2cm to give them maximum moistness and also at an angle.

The outer line is trimmed with a peeler and they are cooked in a light syrup and then lightly roasted in butter to give them a crunchy skin.

6	large peeled and sliced carrots
500ml	water
125g	butter
75g	sugar
	thyme

bay leaves
sea salt
ground white pepper

Method

Bring all the ingredients to the boil and simmer for 6-8 minutes. Leave to cool in the liquor.

When cold, drain and lightly pan fry until you get a slight golden-brown skin. Reserve in a warm area.

Ingredients – the cabbage

1	savoy cabbage
50g	good quality butter

Method

Trim the very green outer leaves and discard them. Cut the nice pale green leaves and simmer them gently in salted water.

When cooked, refresh in ice water and reserve in the fridge.

Ingredients – the sauce

	a dash of olive oil
800g	chopped guinea fowl bones
2	roughly diced carrots
1	roughly diced celery stick
1	large chopped banana shallot
750ml	Monbazillac sweet wine
500ml	veal stock
500ml	guinea fowl stock (or chicken stock)
150g	double cream
50g	raw foie gras

Method

In a deep pan, heat the olive oil and fry the bones to golden brown.

Add the vegetables and continue frying again until brown.

Deglaze with the sweet wine and reduce until syrupy. Add both stocks and bring to the boil. Simmer for 1 hour and pass through a conical sieve, then muslin cloth. Reduce until sticky.

Add 150ml of double cream and bring to the boil again. Add 50g of raw foie gras and with a hand blender, blitz to emulsify.

Correct the seasoning with salt, pepper and a big pinch of sugar. Add a dash of Monbazillac wine to liven it up. Keep aside.

You can make this sauce the day before. Store it in the fridge but do not incorporate the foie gras: rejoin the recipe from there.

To cook and dress

In a non-stick frying pan, with a dash of olive oil, colour the Guinea crowns meticulously and once golden brown all over bake at 190c until the core reaches 65c on a meat thermometer, which takes about 20 minutes. Rest for 10 minutes before slicing.

In another non-stick frying, oven-friendly pan, with a dash of olive oil colour the rolled leg on 4 sides and bake for 10 minutes, turning frequently and basting them from time to time. Insert a meat thermometer until the core reaches 45c. Rest by the crown for 8 minutes.

Heat up a 3rd frying pan and lighly colour the boudin blanc. Bake for 4 minutes on one side and turn over, cooking for a further 2 minutes. When ready place with the crown and rolled leg.

Warm the sauce in a saucepan. Heat up the lentils. Lightly pan fry the carrots and butter the cabbage. Put a non-stick pan on the gas for the foie gras.

Dress the vegetables attractively on the plate and with a boning knife detach the breasts from the bone and trim neatly. Slice them in diamonds shape and place on the cabbage.

Cut a 1.5cm slice of the leg and arrange neatly close to the breast; this is all about heat retention. Now season and with a fork decisively criss cross a 30g slice of premium quality foie gras.

On a medium heat, start pan frying the foie gras. Trim the extremities of the boudin blanc in 2 and place next to the other meats.

Turn the foie gras over and let the residual heat carry on cooking it.

With a blender, whizz the sauce to emulsify and check for sweetness, acidity, seasoning and finally flavour. Correct as required.

Place the foie gras on the top and pour the sauce all over. Serve right away.

ROASTED GRESSINGHAM DUCK BREAST, RHUBARB CONFIT, SHALLOT TATIN, CELERIAC PUREE, LIQUORICE JUS

Yield – 4 portions

> We are big fans of duck at The Checkers and this particular dish showcases the great versatility of this bird.
>
> Paired with an aromatic sweet and sour sauce and contrasting texture, with a crispy shallot tatin, it makes the perfect substitute for beef on a Sunday lunch.

Equipment

Sous vide machine
Hand blender

Ingredients – the Gressingham duck breasts

2	large Gressingham duck breasts
250g	rock salt
250g	duck fat

Method

With a sharp boning knife, score the fat on the top as much as possible, making sure not to reach the flesh. Remove fillet and keep for a different recipe. Trim sinew at the start of the wing. Roll the breasts in rock salt and leave to cure for 15 minutes.

Clean thoroughly under water and place in a sous vide bag with the duck fat. Close tightly and precook in the sous vide for 2 hours at 51c. When done, refresh the whole bag in ice water and store in fridge until needed.

Ingredients – the rhubarb

100g	caster sugar
200g	water
100ml	red grenadine
1	orange peel
1	stick of Tahitian vanilla cut in half lengthways
2	peeled large stick of champagne rhubarb cut into 5cm sticks with pointed extremities

Method

In a medium saucepan, bring the sugar, water, grenadine, orange peel and vanilla to the boil. Add the rhubarb and cook for 2-3 minutes. Take off the heat and cover with a lid. Leave to cool. It must be flavourful and with a slight bite to it. Store in a container in the fridge.

Ingredients – sauce

150g	clear honey
200g	red wine vinegar
330ml	veal stock
660ml	duck stock
30g	liquorice root, put in sous vide bag and smash with a kitchen hammer
80ml	grenadine syrup

Method

In a large saucepan, colour the honey to a dark caramel. Deglaze the vinegar and reduce until syrupy. Add stock and liquorice root reduce to a single cream-like consistency. Finish with grenadine. Pass the sauce through a conical sieve and then through a muslin cloth. Taste for seasoning and correct if necessary. Store in the fridge in a container.

ROASTED GRESSINGHAM DUCK BREAST, RHUBARB CONFIT, SHALLOT TATIN, CELERIAC PUREE, LIQUORICE JUS continued

Ingredients – shallot tatin

This adaptable recipe works well with beef or can also be served on it's own as a funky veggie dish too, so don't be too afraid to make lots of them.

Prepare the shallots

10 large banana shallots

Method

With a small serrated kitchen knife, peel the banana shallots and cut them in 3cm slices. Insert 2 toothpicks arranged as a cross. Reserve.

Ingredients – cooking liquor for shallots

1l	water
250ml	red wine
250g	sugar
35g	fine table salt
	thyme
	bay leaves

Method

In a large saucepan, bring all the ingredients to the boil. Submerge the prepared shallots and simmer for 15 minutes.

Leave them to cool in the liquid.

Ingredients – to assemble and cook the tarts

150g	soft butter (beurre pomade)
150g	caster sugar

1 sheet of high quality puff pastry – ready-rolled to 3mm

Method

In a large deep oven-proof frying pan, spread the butter evenly and sprinkle the sugar on the top.

Place the drained shallots, with the toothpick still in, on the sugar, face down.

Place on a moderate heat and caramelise the shallots.

When well coloured, use a toothpick to transfer the caramelised shallots facedown to 4cm diameter plain sided tart moulds.

Discard the toothpicks. Divide the caramel left in the pan between all the tarts. Leave to cool.

While the tarts are cooling, prick the ready-rolled pastry sheet.

With a 7cm diameter plain cutter, cut the chilled pastry.

Put the pastry on top of the tarts one by one and use a spoon handle to tuck the puff pastry discs around the shallots.

Using a pair of sharp scissors, make a hole in the middle of the tart to allow the steam to come out, in order for the pastry to crisp up.

Cook for 15 minutes at 180c.

TO ASSEMBLE

Drizzle some olive oil a non-stick, oven-friendly frying pan and heat it up.

Place the duck breasts, fat side down and colour slightly. Mind the spitting and get rid of the fat in the pan.

Bake the breasts at 180c for 7-10 minutes, depending on your taste. Don't overcook.

Reheat the purée and store in a squeezy bottle. Warm up the sauce. In a wok, fry a few large spinach leaves in fresh butter and season with ground nutmeg, salt and white pepper.

Toss the spinach leaves while cooking with a garlic clove attached at the end of a fork.

Transfer to a tray layed with absorbent paper.

Reheat the tarts in their moulds and heat up some rhubarb sticks in a pan with its cooking liquor.

Place the warm rectangle plate in front of you, drain the spinach and turn the tarts on top.

With a serrated slicing knife, thinly slice the rested duck breasts.

Place attractively on some sautéed spinach.

Place a few rhubarb sticks on the duck breast and squeeze celeriac purée around.

Pour the sauce and decorate the plate with some red vein sorrel leaves.

Serve.

Ingredients – the celeriac purée

1	large peeled and roughly diced celeriac
150m	double cream
	semi-skimmed milk, to cover
	salt
	ground white pepper

Method

Put the celeriac in a medium size pan and cover with milk. Cook on a medium heat until all the milk has evaporated. It can take some time but the flavour is second to none.

Stir from time to time, especially toward the end of the evaporation process as it can catch easily. Add 150ml of double cream and bring to the boil.

Transfer the celeriac to a blender and blitz the celeriac to a fine purée. Pass through a conical sieve and season with fine salt, ground white pepper and a pinch of cayenne. Transfer to a container and store in the fridge.

GRILLED GRESSINGHAM DUCK CROWN, SPICY PINEAPPLE CARAMEL, PAK CHOI, MADEIRA JUS & SHALLOT VINAIGRETTE

Yield – 4 portions

> Few things can match the beauty of a poached, grilled duck breast that is cooked on the crown.
>
> The flavour comes through so well and the contrast between the crispy skin and tender flesh is quite spectacular.
>
> The sweet notes are paired in this recipe with spicy pineapple caramel that is balanced by the sharpness of a cabernet sauvignon, vinegar and shallot dressing.

Ingredients – the duck crown

Order a crown of duck from your butcher.

Duck fat

Method

We confit the crown before grilling. This gives a very moist, flavourful and tender result. However, it is possible to do this dish by just grilling and roasting the crown. Make sure the wishbone is out and dip it in sea salt for 15 minutes and rinse thoroughly. Bake it in duck fat at 56c for 5 hours.

Once cooked, let it cool in the fat. Pull the crown out and reserve in the fridge.

Ingredients – the Madeira base, part of the base for the dressing

500g	2x2 cm chopped duck bones
2	peeled and roughly diced large carrots
2	peeled and roughly chopped shallots
500ml	sweet Madeira wine
1l	of duck stock (or chicken stock)
500ml	veal stock
100ml	sweet Madeira, to finish the sauce

Method

In an oven set at 200c, colour the duck bones in a large roasting tray with some vegetable oil. Once golden, add the vegetables and colour a little more. Pull the tray out of the oven and place on the hob. Deglaze with the Madeira, reduce by half and add the stocks. Bring to the boil and reduce to a simmer.

Cook gently for an hour-and-a-half. Pass the sauce through a conical sieve and twice through a muslin cloth into a large pan. Reduce to the consistency of double cream, so that it's almost glaze-like. Season accordingly and add enough Madeira to taste, but not too much. You want to create a well-balanced sauce where the Madeira and duck flavours are both distinctive.

GRILLED GRESSINGHAM DUCK CROWN, SPICY PINEAPPLE CARAMEL, PAK CHOI, MADEIRA JUS & SHALLOT VINAIGRETTE

Ingredients – the dressing

100g	finely chopped shallots
50ml	cabernet sauvignon vinegar
200ml	Madeira base
250ml	high quality olive oil
25g	chopped tarragon
15g	chopped chives

Method

In a heavy-bottomed saucepan, sweat the shallots in a little olive oil on a low heat until translucent. Add the vinegar and reduce until dry. Add the Madeira base and bring to the boil.

Take off heat and add olive oil. The herbs should only be added before serving, or they will wilt. Keep at room temperature.

THE PINEAPPLE

On a chopping board with a long serrated knife, chop both ends of a ripe pineapple and carefully peel the outer skin.

Remove all the black dots.

Place in a small roasting tray.

Ingredients – the spicy cooking liquor

This liquor recipe has been adapted for 1 pineapple, but if you would like to make more of this versatile ingredient at the same time you can multiply by as many as you like.

250ml	water
150g	demerara sugar
3g	cayenne pepper
2g	mixed spice
5g	sechuan pepper
5	cloves
3	star anise

Method

In a large saucepan, bring all the ingredients to the boil and take off the heat.

Leave to infuse for 15 minutes and pass the liquor through a fine mesh conical sieve. Pour in the roasting tray over the trimmed pineapple.

To cook the pineapple

Bake the pineapple for about 90 minutes in a 180c oven until all the syrup has evaporated and the pineapple is well caramelised.

Roll it through the liquor every 5-7 minutes or so. When cooked through and golden brown, take out of the oven and cool at room temperature.

When cool enough to handle, cut the pineapple into 4 and remove the core. Cut into 4x2 cm chunks and reserve until needed.

Ingredients – pak choi

2   heads of pak choi cabbage
           fresh butter

Method

Remove the bottom of the cabbage and detach the pak choi leaves. Pre-cook them for 5-10 seconds in a pan of salted boiling water. Refresh straight away in ice water. When cold, drain, trim the bottom of the leaf and reserve in the fridge.

Ingredients – rosti potatoes

The potato selection is vitally important on this recipe. Maris Piper is the spud of choice, but Greek are a good substitute.

250g   of freshly clarified salted butter
1   large peeled Maris Piper
           fine table salt

Method

Using a sharp mandolin, slice the potatoes lengthways and using a chopping knife julienne them finely. When done, put the potatoes in a clean kitchen cloth and pick up the 4 corners. Twist gently to extract as much water as possible.

When dry, place in a bowl and add a little of the clarified butter. Lightly season with salt. In a small frying pan, pour a little clarified butter over the top and arrange your potatoes in a thin and regular fashion.

Put on the heat at a steady pace and cook thoroughly until golden and crisp. Reserve on a wire rack in a dry place.

ASSEMBLING THE DISH

Heat up your cast iron griddle pan and leave it to get really hot, this can take up to 30 minutes, depending on the thickness of the pan.

Criss-cross a nice pattern on the crown and finish the duck in the oven at 180c.

While the duck cooks, heat up the pineapple chunks in a cast iron dish in the oven.

Heat some Madeira sauce and warm through the dressing in another pan.

Lightly sweat the trimmed pak choi leaves in some fresh butter.

Using a sharp boning knife, take the breasts from the crown and trim the sinew by the wings.

Slice 8 neat thin slices from each breast.

Lay 4 warm plates in front of you and arrange the buttered and seasoned pak choi on each plate.

Arrange the warmed-up pineapple pieces at the top of the plate.

Place the slices of duck breast on top of the pak choi

Place a disc of rosti next to it then pour a little Madeira glaze over the duck breasts with the warm dressing.

Serve.

STUFFED SADDLE OF FARMED RABBIT, WITH SHOULDER CONFIT AND TARRAGON, FLAGEOLET BEANS AND JUS A L' ESTRAGON

Yield – 4 portions (as part of taster menu)

Over the years we have cooked rabbit in a lot of different ways and this recipe stands out because because it uses everything from the shoulder to the legs.

It works perfectly with tarragon and also gives us the opportunity to use our knife skills because precision and a sharp knife are called for.

Equipment
Sous vide machine
Kenwood Major mixing bowl

Butchery

Lay the rabbit on the chopping board and clean out the lungs then pick out the kidneys. Pull the shoulder slightly away from the body.

With a sharp boning knife, cut them out and dip them in rock salt for 60 minutes. When the time is up, wash and dry them. Transfer to a tray lined with a clean kitchen cloth. Reserve in the fridge.

Following the back bone, detach the legs, debone them and trim the fat and sinew. Keep the bones in a stainless steel bowl and put the leg meat in a separate container. Keep them both in the fridge.

Split the rabbit carcass in two, straight after the first chop, and carefully separate the rabbit loin from the saddle, keeping the skin attached.

Peel the skin carefully from the loin. Check for any bones or cartilage left over and put the skin between 2 pieces of cling film. Flatten with a rolling pin and keep in the fridge.

Trim the loin from the sinew and keep it in a tray with a bit of olive oil to keep it moist. Put these bones together with the leg bones in a bowl in the fridge.

With a hand held peeler, scrape the bones inside the rib cage and detach the best end from the spine using sharp kitchen scissors. French trim the cutlets neatly. Place them alongside the loin in the oil.

The confit shoulders

Method

Put the salted shoulder and a generous amount of back fat in a sous vide bag and close it tightly.

Cook at 85c for 5 hours. Rather than sous vide, you can put the salted shoulder in an oven-friendly pan and fill up with olive oil, 2 heads of garlic and 2 large tied sprigs of thyme. Bake at 85c for 4 hours.

When the meat falls off the bones it is cooked. Leave to completely cool in the fat, then pick through the meat. Ensure all the bones and cartilage are removed.

Discard the bones and cartilage and reserve the meat in the fridge in a covered container.

Ingredients – the farce

200g	diced flesh of rabbit legs and the weight of the picked confit rabbit shoulder (80-100g)
150g	diced chilled back fat (no skin)
150g	double cream
25cl	red port
25cl	cognac
10g	neatly diced tarragon
	table salt
	pepper
	cayenne
	ground white pepper

Method

Marinade the rabbit, the fat and the alcohol for 24 hours.

In a kitchen grinder, pass the diced rabbit legs, back fat cubes and marinade liquor to a Kenwood mixing bowl.

Add the confit shoulders and pour in the cream. With the K paddle attachment, beat thoroughly and season accordingly.

Pan fry a little piece to check on the consistency and seasoning.

When perfect, transfer to a disposable piping bag and reserve in the fridge.

Ingredients – the spinach

1	bag of spinach

Method

Select the biggest and greenest spinach leaves from the pack and blanch them for 10 seconds in boiling water. Refresh immediately in iced water and lay on a kitchen cloth.

Cover and store in the fridge until needed.

STUFFED SADDLE OF FARMED RABBIT, WITH SHOULDER CONFIT AND TARRAGON, FLAGEOLET BEANS AND JUS A L' ESTRAGON continued

Assembling the stuffed saddle

Method

Open the cling film and season both sides of the belly skin with salt. Place the trimmed fillet at the top and lay the spinach without leaving any spaces in it.

Pipe as much farce as the size of the loin will allow and close it. Now wrap this stuffed saddle in 2 rounds of crepinette and with some butcher string tie it neatly, like a roti.

Keep it in the fridge until needed.

Ingredients – the sauce

All	the bones (carcass and legs) chopped at about 0.5cm
2	roughly diced carrots
2	peeled and roughly chopped banana shallots
250ml	white wine
500ml	chicken stock
500ml	veal stock
150g	tarragon

Method

Add a little oil to a large frying pan and colour the bones until golden brown. Add the vegetables and carry on cooking a bit more, for approximately 2 minutes.

Deglaze with the white wine and reduce by half. Add the stocks. Bring to the boil and skim thoroughly.

Simmer for 1 hour and pass through a conical sieve, then through a folded muslin cloth over a large pan. Reduce at full gas until it reaches the consistency of single cream.

When ready, add the tarragon and infuse for 15 minutes. Pass through a conical sieve again and correct the seasoning. Reserve in the fridge.

Ingredients – flageolet beans

500g	flageolet beans (soaked 24h in water prior to cooking)
1	large peeled onion
2	large peeled carrots
1	large bouquet garni
	white chicken stock, to cover
	fine table salt
	ground white pepper

Method

Bring all the ingredients to the boil and simmer gently for 2 hours. Taste and correct the cooking and seasoning accordingly, it may take longer to cook. Discard the bouquet garni and add 100g of fresh butter at the end. Transfer to a container. Store in the fridge.

To Assemble

Heat a non-stick, oven-friendly pan and add a splash of olive oil. Season and sear the saddle on each of its 4 sides. Bake at 180c for 10-12 minutes. To be sure it is cooked, insert a needle through the middle and leave it for 6 seconds. Remove and check the needle is warm. When warm, take the saddle out of the oven – the residual heat while resting will complete the cooking process. While the saddle is cooking, heat up the flageolet in a saucepan and the sauce in a tea pot. Warm a non-stick frying pan and roast the best end gently for 2 minutes.

Leave to rest in a warm place. Lay 4 warm bowls, taste and correct the seasoning and divide the flageolet beans between the 4 bowls. With a pair of sharp scissors cut the string from the saddle and with a sharp serrated carving knife cut the extremities. Cut the saddle in the middle.

Place the meat on the beans and cut the best end in 4. Put on the plate. Taste the hot sauce and correct the seasoning if necessary. Pour the sauce and serve.

GRILLED LOIN OF HARE, CUISSE A LA ROYALE, TRANCHE DE LARD FUME, CHESTNUT AND WHITE PORT PURÉE, JUS DE CUISSON AU GENIEVRE

Yield – 4 portions

In Powys, there is an abundance of shooting during game season.

From pheasant to hare and from teal to grouse, there is always something available.

Hunters and shooters are always very keen to offer us their harvest.

In this recipe we use all parts of the hare.

We feel that in doing this, we are showing the greatest respect to this beautiful animal.

Equipment

Meat grinder
Sharp secateurs
Sous vide machine
Combi oven
Tall jug blender

Ingredients – the hare and marinade

1	hare
	olive oil
	handful fresh thyme
2	heads of garlic

The butchery

Using a sharp boning knife, place the tip behind the ilium bone and follow carefully along it.

Twist gently to detach the back legs and put them on a clean stainless steel tray.

Pull the shoulder away from the side and again cut delicately behind them.

Place them on the tray.

Turn the hare over and cut it in two, just 1 rib before the saddle.

With the knife-edge, cut between the loin and the spine

and separate them. Keep everything tidy and on the tray.

Slightly detach the best end loin from the remaining spine and with a pair of sharp secateurs, split the cutlet from the spine.

Trim the best end and submerge in a mix of olive oil, 2 garlic heads, halved, and a handful of fresh thyme.

Trim the fat saddle loins and marinate them for 24-48 hours with the trimmed best end.

On a chopping board cut the leg from the inside and work your way around the bone, trying to keep it as whole as possible.

Once done, trim the skin as you would if you were skinning a fish.

Finally place the whole trimmed leg flesh between 2 sheets of cling film and flatten them with a kitchen hammer.

Reserve in the fridge.

Chop all the remaining bones for the sauce and stock.

159

GRILLED LOIN OF HARE, CUISSE A LA ROYALE, TRANCHE DE LARD FUME, CHESTNUT AND WHITE PORT PURÉE, JUS DE CUISSON AU GENIEVRE continued

The farce Royale (to stuff the leg)

Ingredients – list A

40g	finely chopped sweated banana shallots with
5g	crushed garlic
250g	hare flesh trimmings plus the liver, heart, cheeks, lungs and tongue
150g	diced pork flesh
200g	pork fat

Ingredients – list B

50g	small dice of streaky smoked bacon
75g	fresh breadcrumbs
2	whole egg
50g	red port
25g	cognac
30g	chopped flat parsley

Method

In a large stainless steel bowl mix the ingredients from List A then pass through a meat grinder. Then combine with the ingredients from List B with a spatula. Put in a disposable piping bag and reserve in the fridge.

On a flat surface, lay 2 layers of cling film on top of each other and sprinkle with salt, pepper and a squeeze of olive oil.

Place the hare leg in the middle of it and pipe the farce on top. Roll it and close it tightly. Repeat the operation with all the remaining legs.

Cook in a sous vide machine for 6 hours 30 minutes at 59c. Refresh right away in ice water.

On a piece of cling film, lay a neat square of thinly sliced smoked streaky bacon.

Place the cooked leg on and roll the bacon around it.

Leave in the fridge until needed.

The baked smoked streaky tranche

In a combi oven, bake a whole side of smoked streaky submerged in chicken stock for 10 hours at 98c. When cooked, leave it to cool in the liquid. When cold, pull the belly out of the liquid, wrap it in cling film and press between 2 flat trays with a weight on top. The smoked stock can be used for another recipe like a risotto or a lentil dish.

The following day, trim the skin and slice lengthways, 1x4x12cm. Reserve in the fridge.

Ingredients – the chestnut and white port purée

250g	warmed peeled chestnuts (you can warm them in the bag in simmering water for 25 minutes, they are available from any good supermarket)
200g	water
2g	fine salt
20g	caster sugar
5g	agar agar powder
100g	white port

Method

Place the warm chestnuts into a tall jug blender. In a tall-sided pan, heat up the water and add the sugar, salt and agar-agar powder until boiling.

Tip it in while the blender is running. Finally add the white port and mix until it's very smooth. Pass through a fine mesh kitchen tamis and set aside until needed. Work quickly as the purée crusts almost immediately. Reserve in the fridge.

DISH ASSEMBLY

Heat up a non-stick, oven-friendly frying pan and roast the leg for 12 minutes, three on each of the four sides.

Add the thick slice of smoked bacon for the last 4 minutes, two minutes on each side. Heat up the grill until really hot and criss-cross the best end and loin. Keep warm.

Warm up the cabbage in melted butter and place the smoked streaky next to it on a warm plate.

Slice the leg, carve the fillet, trim the best end and dress nicely on the cabbage.

Squeeze some chestnut purée attractively on the plate and serve with some horseradish-pommes mousseline and the sauce on the side.

Ingredients – the juniper sauce

1kg	of 1cm x 1cm chopped hare bones
2	roughly chopped carrots
1	roughly diced chopped onion
1	roughly chopped celery stick
100g	brandy
100g	red port
1000g	red wine
25g	white wine vinegar
1.5l	veal stock
1.5lt	game stock, or chicken stock if unavailable
5g	orange peel
3	cloves
12g	crushed juniper berry
50g	thyme
80g	roughly chopped garlic head

Method

In a deep, tall pan, roast the hare bones until well coloured. Add the vegetables and colour a little bit more, for about two minutes. Add the brandy and the port and boil for 1 minute. Add the red wine and the vinegar and reduce by half. Add the stocks, orange peel and cloves and simmer for 1 hour and 30 minutes.

Pass through a conical sieve then pass through a muslin cloth. Reduce the sauce until it has the consistency of single cream.

Place the garlic, thyme, and crushed juniper berries in the sauce and infuse for 10 minutes. Pass through a conical sieve and reserve in the fridge.

STUFFED SADDLE OF WELSH LAMB, TOMATO FARCIES, GRILLED ASPARAGUS, SAUCE PALOISE & ROSEMARY JUS

Yield – 4 portions

> There are few dishes that capture the flavours of spring as well as this.
>
> Moist, tender and sweet spring lamb is beautifully paired with seasonal asparagus with a rich Sauce Paloise providing a delightful accompaniment.
>
> Stuffed tomatoes add colour, flavour and texture while an intense rosemary jus makes it the complete main course.

Ingredients – fillet

1	loin of lamb – fat and fillet attached

Butchery

With a sharp butcher's knife, debone the loin of lamb, leaving the skin on and free up the little fillet under.

Chop the bones for the sauce, split the meat from the fat, and trim all fat and sinew. Reserve on a tray in the fridge.

Trim the fat into a paper thin, 15cm square and keep in the fridge until needed.

Ingredients – confit shoulder

1	shoulder of lamb
	some rock salt
	duck fat
1	garlic head

Method

Put the shoulder into the rock salt for 2 hours then rinse it under water and bake in duck fat in a low oven for 4 hours at 90c, along with the garlic head.

It will be cooked when the meat falls easily off the bone. Leave to cool in the fat. Once cold, peel the meat away from the bone.

Ingredients – lamb mousse

100g	lean lamb meat
200g	double cream
60g	egg white
25g	wholegrain mustard
	salt
	pepper
	cayenne

Method

In a food processor, puree the lamb flesh and the egg white until very smooth.

Add the seasoning then slowly add the cold double cream. Pass through a fine mesh drum and reserve in fridge.

For the lamb filling, combine one third of lamb mousse and two thirds of lamb confit.

Mix, add the grain mustard and season well, then roll with the small lamb fillet in the middle.

To roll the lamb, lay out the square of fat, then the trimmed cannon of meat, then the filling and roll the lamb.

Wrap in crepinette (pork cawl) and tie up with butcher's string. Reserve in the fridge.

164

STUFFED SADDLE OF WELSH LAMB, TOMATO FARCIES, GRILLED ASPARAGUS, SAUCE PALOISE & ROSEMARY JUS continued

Ingredients – tomato

6	large tomatoes on the vine, peeled
1	head of garlic
2	sprigs of thyme
10g	sugar
	salt and pepper to taste
4	spoons of aged balsamic vinegar
12	spoons of virgin olive oil

Method

With a serrated knife, cut the top off the tomatoes and empty them: a melon baller works really well.

Mix all the garlic, thyme, sugar, salt, pepper, balsamic vinegar and olive oil together in a big deep bowl and then roll the tomato thoroughly through it.

Lay the tomatoes on a baking sheet and cook at 60c for 4 hours. Keep warm.

Ingredients – asparagus

16	asparagus spears

Method

Peel the asparagus and tie with butcher's string in a bundle of 8. Poach in salted water at a low simmer for 10 minutes, so that they are tender but have a bite.

Once cooked refresh in iced water, drain and reserve in the fridge.

Ingredients – jus

Chopped	lamb bones
2	shallots
1	carrot

300ml	white wine to deglaze
1l	veal stock
2l	lamb stock

Method

Roast the bones until golden and add the shallots and carrot.

Cook a little more, then deglaze with the white wine and reduce till syrupy. Add the stocks and cook for 1 hour.

Pass through a conical sieve and muslin cloth. Reduce the consistency so that it coats the back of the spoon.

Infuse with chopped up garlic and a rosemary sprig for 10 minutes then pass again.

Reserve in a small pot with a lid.

Ingredients – sauce paloise

Reduce 20cl of white wine with 10 cl of white wine vinegar, 10 mint sprigs and 12 black peppercorn. Add 3 egg yolks and beat over a bain marie until light and frothy.

Off the heat, add 250g of clarified butter and check the seasoning, adding salt and pepper.

If it is too tart, add a squeeze of lemon juice and pass through a muslin cloth, keep warm.

To serve

Roast the lamb at 180c to the desired pinkness and rest.

While the lamb is resting, grill the asparagus on a hot grill.

Pan fry a few spinach leaves and fill the warm tomatoes with them. Attractively arrange the asparagus inside and close the tomato lid.

BARBECUED BEST END OF WELSH LAMB, AUBERGINE AND CUMIN PURÉE, GRILLED COURGETTE, LAMB SHOULDER CROUSTILLANT ROSEMARY JUS

Yield – 4 portions

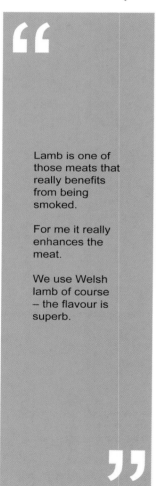

Lamb is one of those meats that really benefits from being smoked.

For me it really enhances the meat.

We use Welsh lamb of course – the flavour is superb.

Equipment

Chinese spiralizer
Combi oven
Tall jug blender
Mandolin

Ingredients – braised lamb shoulder and braising jus

1	shoulder of lamb	5	large diced tomatoes
1	diced onion	200g	dry white wine
1	large head	1l	of lamb stock or
	of garlic cut in 2		chicken stock
2	large carrots cut	0.5l	veal stock
	into wheels	1	large rosemary bunch
1	roughly diced celery		tied with kitchen string

Method

In a hot frying pan, using some olive oil, colour the shoulder until golden brown and transfer into an oven friendly dish alongside the stocks. In a different pan, heat more olive oil and fry the onions, garlic, carrots and celery until they get a good colour. Deglaze with the white wine and reduce by half.

Add the tomatoes. Transfer the vegetables next to the shoulder and bring to the boil. Skim. Lay a piece of baking parchment that has been cut down to size on the top. Close with a fitting lid or a doubled piece of foil paper then bake for 12 hours at 85c in an oven with the fan on full blast. When cooked, the meat should be falling off the bone. Leave to cool in the liquid.

When completely cold, pull the 3 bones and pick through the meat. Discard the fatty bits and reserve the picked meat in the fridge. Pass the cooking juice through a fine mesh conical sieve and throw away the vegetables. Pass again through a muslin cloth and reduce to a texture similar to single cream. Infuse with a generous amount of rosemary and 2 heads of roughly chopped garlic. Leave to infuse for 10 minutes and pass through a chinois again.

166

BARBECUED BEST END OF WELSH LAMB, AUBERGINE AND CUMIN PURÉE, GRILLED COURGETTE, LAMB SHOULDER CROUSTILLANT ROSEMARY JUS continued

Ingredients – rolling the braised shoulder meat in potatoes

Two/three Maris Piper potatoes

Method

When the sauce is finished, use some of it to bind the braised shoulder meat. In a piece of cling film roll into a 2cm diameter sausage and set in the fridge.

When cold and firm, cut into a 5cm tube. Unwrap the cling film and wrap the pancake (recipe page 136) around it.

Using a Chinese spiralizer, make some spaghetti from Maris Piper potatoes and pre-cook them 1 at the time in the fryer at 110c for a few seconds.

While still warm, wrap them twice neatly around the meaty-pancake and keep in the fridge.

Ingredients – butcher the best end of lamb

3   best end of lamb

Method

French trim the best end leaving the fat on the eye. Dip in rock salt for 15 minutes, rinse thoroughly and keep in the fridge. Trim in sinew and wrap every bone individually with some foil.

Light up your barbecue with a generous heapful of charcoal and leave it to burn for 30 minutes.

When incandescent, place your lamb on the rack, fat-side down, and leave on until well-smoked, especially the fat. Do not let the flames burn the meat and fat.

While the smoking goes on, brown 200g of fresh butter in a pan and add 2 chopped garlic heads and a generous handful of thyme.

When the lamb is well smoked, transfer into an oven tray and pour the brown butter and aromates onto the meat. Finish to cook it in the Combi oven set on mixed heat (4%humidity) at 58c with the fan on full, to achieve medium rare.

Leave until the core of the meat reaches 58c, which should take 1-2 hours.

Ingredients – aubergine purée

3	large aubergines
20g	chopped garlic
	cumin powder
3	large sprigs of thyme and a bay leaf
	fine salt and ground white pepper
150ml	cream reduced to 90g
6g	of high quality of agar-agar powder

Method

Lay the aubergines on 2 layers of kitchen foil and top and tail them. Cut in 2 lengthways and criss-cross the flesh with a small serrated knife.

Spread the chopped garlic evenly between them.

Dust on a generous amount of cumin powder over and add thyme, bay leaf, fine salt and pepper.

Roll the aubergine in the foil and bake them at 180c for 2-3 hours. When cooked, open the foil and discard the thyme and bay leaf.

Scoop out all of the flesh and half of the skin.

Blitz in a tall blender. Gradually add the warm, reduced double cream until a nice purée consistency is obtained.

Weigh 600g of the aubergine purée and 6g of agar agar powder.

Heat up 200g of it and whisk the powder in. Bring it to the boil and cook for 20 seconds.

Add the remaining 400g of aubergine purée and whisk well.

Transfer in a stainless steel tray and leave to set in the fridge for 2 hours.

When set as jelly, put through the tall blender again and pass through a fine mesh conical sieve.

Warm in a small sauce pan, adjust the seasoning and put into a squeezy bottle.

Keep warm.

To grill the courgettes, turn the gas on full beneath the cast iron grill pan and leave to heat up for 30 minutes.

With a Benriner mandolin, slice 2 courgettes on the highest setting. Season with fine salt and lightly dip in olive oil.

When the grill is hot enough, turn off the gas and criss-cross the seasoned courgette. If the grill is super-hot, that should take about 4 seconds on each stripe. Put the grilled courgette on a chopping board and trim the end off.

Reserve in a warm dish.

TO ASSEMBLE

Turn on the fryer and set it to 180c. Dip the braised shoulder croustillants in and set your timer on 3 minutes 30 seconds.

That is time you have to dress the plates.

Warm up the sauce.

On some warm plates, squeeze a point of warm aubergine purée and skilfully swoosh it with the back of a spoon. Arrange the warm, grilled courgettes.

Carve the best end and place on top of the courgette.

Pour the sauce in the aubergine puree and on the lamb and serve straight away.

GRILLED VEAL KIDNEYS AND POMMES PONT-NEUF COOKED IN KIDNEYS FAT, ONIONS PURÉE SAUCE RAVIGOTE

Yield – 6 portions

This is a very flavoursome dish comprising wonderful chips and a simple onion puree complemented by crispy shallots and a mustard and herb dressing.

It is served alongside delicious veal kidneys.

It features all of the ingredients for a perfect lunch sur la terrasse!

Equipment

Mandolin
Tall jug blender
Dehydrator
Sous vide machine

Ingredients – onions purée

5	peeled large white onions
250g	salted butter
150g	double cream

Method

With a mandolin, slice all the onions on the thinnest setting and cook in a large pan with the butter very gently for 3-4 hours. They have to create their own caramel and be thoroughly cooked so that they turn slightly brown. When cooked, drain the onions over a colander and discard the butter.

Put back in the pan with the double cream and bring to the boil. Transfer to a tall blender and blitz for 2 minutes. Pass the purée through a fine mesh conical sieve. Correct the seasoning and store in a plastic container in the fridge until needed.

Ingredients – crispy shallots

2	peeled large banana shallots
1	pot of plain flour

Method

Slice the shallots at 3mm sideways using a mandolin. Discard the middle in order to gain nice neat circles. Roll in flour and deep fry in vegetable oil at 180c. When cooked and crispy, season lightly with fine salt and keep in a dehydrator or airtight container until needed.

Ingredientrs – sauce ravigotte

35g	Dijon mustard
75g	white wine vinegar
500ml	vegetable oil
60g	finely chopped capers
60g	crushed diced cornichons
60g	chopped parsley
60g	chopped tarragon
60g	chopped chervil
60g	finely chopped and rinsed shallots
8g	fine table salt
3g	ground white pepper
2g	ground cayenne pepper
20g	lemon juice

Method

In a stainless steel bowl, whisk the mustard, vinegar and pour in the oil slowly, like a mayonnaise.

When emulsified, add all the other ingredients and taste. Adjust the acidity and the seasoning if necessary. Transfer to a container and keep in the fridge.

Ingredients – veal kidneys

3   veal kidneys
        table salt

Method

Detach all the fat from the fresh kidneys. Put 3/4 of the fat through the kitchen grinder and over a large pan bring it to the boil and render.

When completely melted pass through a chinois in another deep pan and keep on the side for a later stage.

Roughly dice the remaining fat and store in the fridge.

Season the kidneys with table salt and cook them sous vide with a bit of their own fat at 55c for 30 minutes.

Ingredients – chips preparation

3kg   peeled Maris piper potatoes cut into chunks
        of 2x2x6cm

Method

In a pan of salted water, bring potatoes to the boil and cook until the side gets fluffy. Drain and dry in a cloth.

To assemble

Put the cast iron griddle pan full blast on the gas and bring the kidney fat to 180c. Cook the chips until crispy and season with Maldon sea salt immediately. Cook the diced kidney fat gently in a hot frying pan until crispy and keep on the wire rack. Open the kidney bag and drain. Put the pre-cooked kidneys on a chopping board and with a sharp knife cut 1cm slices. Put in a bowl with olive oil, season and grill 2 by 2 on the griddle pan until a nice pattern is obtained. Transfer to a wire rack and rest for 3 minutes. Heat the onion purée and warm up the sauce.

Lay your warm board in front of you and place your chips randomly. Scatter a few crispy kidney fat pieces on the chips and the grilled kidneys in the middle. Add shallot rings and serve with onion purée and the sauce, served in a warm bowl on the side.

ROAST RIB OF BEEF WITH OXTAIL-STUFFED FONDANTES, SPRING ONIONS CARAMEL AND SAUCE AU VIN ROUGE

Yield – 6-10 portions

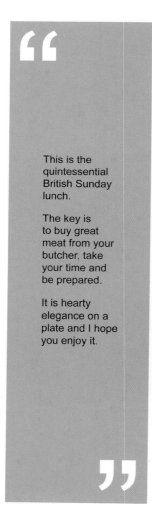

"

This is the quintessential British Sunday lunch.

The key is to buy great meat from your butcher, take your time and be prepared.

It is hearty elegance on a plate and I hope you enjoy it.

"

Ingredients – rib of beef

Ask your butcher for a well hung (36 days) fore rib of beef.

The size depends on how many and how hungry your guests are. We suggest roughly 2-3 portions per rib.

We use Celtic Pride beef and only ever have had brilliant feedback from guests.

Method

Season the rib generously with salt then place the whole rib in a hot frying pan with some olive oil, colour the fat and once golden brown transfer to a roasting tray.

Bake at 57c for 14 hours on a combi setting with 5% humidity.

With a digital thermometer probe the center of the meat and it should read 57c for medium rare.

Leave to rest in the oven.

ROAST RIB OF BEEF WITH OXTAIL-STUFFED FONDANTES, SPRING ONIONS CARAMEL AND SAUCE AU VIN ROUGE continued

POTATO FONDANTS, OXTAIL AND SAUCE

Ingredients

12	potatoes, allowing 2 per person
80ml	water
200g	salted butter
200g	unsalted butter

Method

Select a waxy potato, like desiree, and with a 6cm plain cutter, cut neat circles of 3cm high.

With a Parisian scoop, dig a hole in the middle and run a peeler alongside the edges to give them a smoother look.

Place face-up in a pan and add a bit of water (to a depth of 2cm) which helps to melt the butter evenly. Add the 2 different sorts of butter on a high heat.

Bring to the boil and cook until the colour of the potatoes is golden brown.

Take off the heat and rest the potatoes and brown butter for 5 minutes.

With a palette knife, turn them over and finish by confiting them in the butter at a very low heat, or eventually in an oven for 60-90mn at 140c dry heat.

Cook until completely soft, but with the shape held.

Reserve in the butter until needed.

Ingredients – oxtail stuffing and sauce

See recipe for braised oxtail pithiviers on page 176.

Method

When the potatoes are cooked and the oxtail warm and well seasoned, tip out the remaining butter in the hole and stuff them generously.

Sprinkle a bit of freshly grated parmesan and colour until golden brown under the salamander, or grill, and keep warm.

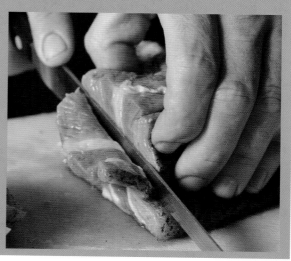

Ingredients – spring onions

25-30	spring onions
200g	butter
100g	water
25g	sugar
	salt

Method

Top and tail the spring onions and trim the outer leaf of each one.

Place in a shallow pan with butter, water and sugar and season with salt accordingly.

Bring to the boil and caramelise the onions.

Once coloured take off the heat and keep in the cooking pan in a warm place.

Ingredients – girolles

500g	small Scottish girolles
2	banana shallots
25g	finely chopped parsley
	fine table salt
	ground white pepper
	knob of butter

Method

Scrape the outside of each mushroom stalk and wash them at least 3 times in a bath of clean fresh water.

Use a spoon with holes to take them out and don't leave them too long in the water as they act like a sponge and boil rather than fry.

Ingredients – spinach for 6 people

250g large leaf spinach
30g high quality diced salted butter

Method

In a hot wok or frying pan, place the butter quickly followed by the spinach.

Cook for 1-2 minutes and toss using a garlic clove spiked at the end of a fork. Season with salt, pepper and ground nutmeg. When just cooked, transfer to a perforated tray to drain the juice and keep warm.

DISH ASSEMBLY

Assemble all your garnishes and heat up the sauce. Bring the beef to the table and slice with a fork and a sharp knife.

ROASTED BEEF FILLET, BRAISED OXTAIL PITHIVIERS

Yield – 6 portions

> We almost always have some sort of oxtail on the menu because it is incredibly delicious and also creates one of the best beef sauces ever.
>
> Pithiviers are the perfect pairing and have all the hallmarks of great gastronomy: crispy pastry, juicy and flavourful fillings and indulgent foie gras.
>
> This, then, is classic Checkers braised oxtail and sauce.

Braised oxtail and sauce

It is difficult to braise oxtail in small quantities but any leftovers can be served on its own with mousseline and fat lardons – or you could make a lot of pithiviers and freeze.

Ingredients

2	large oxtails (3kg) cut between the bones
1.5l	cooking red wine
750ml	of brandy
3	roughly diced large carrots
2	peeled roughly diced onions
1	head of celery roughly chopped
2lt	veal stock
1lt	chicken stock
1	pig trotter
250g	butter
80g	multi-purpose flour
300ml	of red wine
4	heads of garlic, roughly chopped
1	large bouquet of thyme

Method

The day before, make the sauce.

Marinate the oxtail, carrots, onions and celery in the red wine in a plastic container and keep in the fridge. The next day, drain the meat and vegetables in a colander over a large oven-friendly baking tray. Move the colander and reduce the red wine by half. Add the stocks and the pig trotter and bring to the boil. Now heat 2 large frying pans and roast the seasoned oxtail and marinated vegetables until golden brown in olive oil.

Deglaze with the cognac. Transfer everything in the baking tray alongside the other ingredients. Bring to the boil, skim and cover with a piece of baking parchment. Close the tray with a tight-fitting lid or a sheet of foil. Bake at 98c with a dry heat and full fan for 10-12 hours, until the meat falls off the bones.

Cool in the liquid. When cold, pick through the tail and trotter. Making sure no bones are left, keep the meat in a container in the fridge. Bring the jellified sauce back to the boil and pass it through a conical sieve. Reduce by half. In another saucepan, melt the butter and add the flour.

Cook until you get a brown roux and deglaze with 300ml red wine. Add to the reduced stocks. Bring to the boil and adjust the consistency. Drop in the garlic and thyme and infuse for 15 minutes. Pass through a conical sieve again and correct the seasoning.

Keep in a container in the fridge.

ROASTED BEEF FILLET, BRAISED OXTAIL PITHIVIERS continued

Foie gras

Ingredients for 6 pithiviers

3x50g	good quality Rougie sliced foie gras
	table salt
	ground white pepper
	olive oil

Method

In a hot frying pan squirt some olive oil. Flash fry the seasoned, frozen foie gras until you get a golden brown crust. Take off the heat and store on a plate in the fridge. Cut the slices in half and reserve.

The oxtail filling

Ingredients

40g	freshly diced butter
30g	olive oil
100g	peeled and regularly diced onions
50g	crushed garlic with the germs removed
150g	peeled and regularly diced carrots, brunoise
500g	braised oxtail

Method

In a medium-sized pan, melt the butter and add the olive oil. Add the onions and garlic and cook gently until it gets very soft and confited, which takes about an hour.

Add the carrots and cook for 30 minutes more. Season with salt and pepper and add the oxtail. Mix well and bind with some of the sauce.

Season again and place in a bowl in the fridge.

Putting the pithiviers together

Ingredients – egg wash

5	eggs yolks
150ml	semi-skimmed milk
5g	salt
5g	caster sugar

Method

Blitz all the ingredients with a hand held blender and pass the liquid through a fine mesh conical sieve.

Ingredients – construction

For this stage you will need the pancakes recipe on page 136.

6	disks of good quality puff pastry (12cm diameter)
6	disks of good quality puff pastry (3cm diameter)
6	disks of pancakes (10cm diameter)
6	disks of pancakes (4cm diameter)
	the cooled pan fried foie gras

Method

On a flat surface sift some flour and lay the big puff pastry disc. Brush some egg wash on and lay the big pancake disc.

Egg wash again and spread 70g of braised oxtail mix. Make a hole in the middle and place the foie gras in.

Push the pithiviers in a 6.5cm diameter bowl, that has been previously sifted with flour. Top up with 20g of braised oxtail mix. Flatten the meat, brush some egg wash over and lay the small pancake disc on top.

Finally brush the top of the pancake again with egg wash and lay the small pastry disc on.

Fold the outer puff pastry on the small pastry one, push a little, and turn the bowl over. Store on baking parchment in the freezer. Repeat the operation with the other 5. When all done, brush them with egg wash 3 times, leaving a space of at least 15 minutes between each coat. Keep in the freezer. When all are egg washed and slightly frozen, place them on a turned over stainless steel bowl. Score them one by one, with a sharp turning knife.

Keep on cut-down-to-size baking parchment in the freezer.

Ingredients – the carrots

6	large peeled and sliced carrots
500ml	water
125g	butter
75g	sugar
	thyme
	bay leaves
	sea salt and ground white pepper

Method

Bring all the ingredients to the boil and simmer for 6-8 minutes. Leave to cool in the syrup. When cold, drain and lightly pan fry until you get a slight golden-brown colour. Reserve in a warm area.

Ingredients – prepare the beef

6	200g beef fillet steaks and season

To assemble

Set up your Rational oven on 190c dry heat, with full fan, and insert a baking tray upside down, to facilitate the palette knife sliding under the pithiviers.

Bake the pithiviers for 12 minutes, turning to 180c halfway through. Keep warm.

Now heat up a frying pan and squirt some olive oil in it. Season your steak with salt and pan. Fry until well-coloured. Rare is the recommendation for this fine piece of meat.

When cooked, rest for 5 minutes. Meanwhile, heat the sauce and fry the spinach with nutmeg and salt and pepper, as described on page 175 and heat the carrots.

Lay the warm plates in front of you and place the spinach in a strip. With a carving knife, slice the beef in thin strips. Plate neatly. Arrange the warm carrots and place the pithiviers on the other side of the plate.

Brush the pithiviers with olive oil and serve the sauce on the side.

GRILLED FILLET OF CELTIC PRIDE BEEF, POMMES AU BEURRE, GROS LARDONS FUME, PARSLEY PURÉE, BÉARNAISE

Yield – 6 portions

This is one of my favourite beef recipes.

It is remarkably flavoursome and is served with a fragrant parsley puree and one of our favourite potato sides.

You can use the sauce from page 176 or serve with a béarnaise on the side.

Equipment

Combi oven
Tall jug blender
Mandolin

Ingredients – pommes au beurre

3	large red washed potatoes
500g	butter
1.25l	vegetable oil

Method

Unwrap the butter and put it a plastic jug and cover it with cling film. Melt it in the microwave until the clarified butter sits on top of the milk. Keep the jug in a warm place.

Wash and peel the potatoes, slice them on the highest settings of a Benriner Mandolin. Cut them with a plain 5cm diameter cutter to obtain thick discs.

Season a large pan of water with coarse sea salt and bring to the boil. Dip the discs of potato in it and simmer until cooked, while retaining their bite. Refresh straight away in iced water.

Using a clean tea-towel, dry the potatoes thoroughly. Using dariole moulds measuring 3.5cm diameter by 5cm height, season the potatoes with salt and brush each one with the clarified butter. Build a tower of 12 discs always seasoning and brushing each potato slice before putting it in the stack.

Place the potato-filled darioles in a very flat, oven-friendly tray. Fill the tray to ¾ of the side of the dariole moulds with vegetable oil and bake in the oven at 180c for 45 minutes/ 1 hour. When ready, the potato should be golden with a crispy outer ring and a seasoned soft core.

Turn the darioles over a wire rack, resting on a tray to get rid of unwanted butter. Keep warm.

CHECKERS
main

GRILLED FILLET OF CELTIC PRIDE BEEF, POMMES AU BEURRE, GROS LARDONS FUME, PARSLEY PURÉE, BÉARNAISE continued

Ingredients – parsley puree

500g	washed and dried flat parsley
150g	washed and dried spinach
100g	fresh butter
300g	double cream, reduced to 100g
	ground nutmeg
	fine table salt
	ground white pepper

Method

In a large pan, rapidly boil some seasoned water and blanch the parsley and spinach for 30 seconds. To keep the puree very green, make sure the water boils all the time. Small batches are recommended. Refresh in ice water immediately.

Replace the water in the pan with fresh water and season with salt again. Put the parsley and spinach leaves back on to boil again for 10 minutes, boiling all the time. Drain the parsley and spinach leaves thoroughly to avoid a watery purée. A good way to do that is by placing them in a kitchen cloth and squeezing the juice out by twisting the top.

Place the dry leaves in a tall blender and add the fresh butter then season with fine salt, ground white pepper and ground nutmeg. Start the machine. Boil the reduced cream and pour it over the parsley and spinach. Blitz thoroughly and adjust the consistency to your liking. You might need to reduce the cream a little more, or not, depending on the consistency.

When perfectly smooth, pass through a conical sieve as a precaution. Taste for seasoning and refrigerate.

GROS LARDONS FUME

This recipe is for a whole side of streaky bacon, which might seem a lot.

But if you are a keen cook and gourmand it will be gone in no time.

Ingredients

1	whole side of smoked streaky bacon
	chicken stock to cover, 4l approximately

Method

In a combi oven set on full fan, bake the whole side of smoked streaky submerged in chicken stock for 10 hours at 98c

When cooked leave it to cool in the liquid.

When cold, pull the belly out of the liquid, wrap it in cling film and press between 2 flat trays with a weight on top.

The following day, trim the skin, cut a long thick slice and then chop fat lardons measuring 2cm x2cm x4cm.

Reserve in the fridge.

182

Ingredients – grilled beef

6x	220g Celtic Pride marbled beef fillet
	table salt
	ground pepper
	olive oil

Method

Take the fillet out of the fridge 30 minutes before grilling them.

Roll in olive oil and season with salt.

Ingredients – tarragon reduction

5	peeled and sliced large banana shallots
8g	crushed white peppercorns
100g	of tarragon (1 bunch)
200ml	white wine vinegar
100ml	white wine

Method

Bring all the ingredients to the boil and leave to infuse for 24 hours before using.

Store in a plastic container, with the lid on, in the fridge.

Ingredients – the sauce Béarnaise

50g	of the tarragon reduction
3	egg yolks
250g	fresh butter
15-20g	fresh lemon juice
20g	neatly diced tarragon leaves

Method

Clarify the butter in the microwave and keep warm.

Bring a pan of water to the boil and place a stainless steel bowl over it.

Tip the tarragon reduction in and heat it up.

When warm, whisk the egg in and emulsify until light and fluffy but cooked.

This stage is critical as the texture of the sauce depends on it.

Take the bowl off the heat and place on your worktop with a cloth beneath to hold it in place.

Trickle the warm, clarified butter in gently while whisking all the time.

If too stiff, add a little hot water to the mix.

Taste and correct the seasoning with fine salt and ground white pepper and the acidity with the lemon juice.

Gently mix in the diced tarragon leaves and keep warm.

TO ASSEMBLE

Turn on the heat under a cast iron griddle pan and let it heat up for at least 30 minutes.

While the grill is heating up, warm up the parsley puree and warm up the potatoes.

When super-hot, griddle the seasoned beef steaks and criss-cross nicely.

It should be just rare.

Finish in the oven at 180c for 3-4 minutes.

Dress on a plate with the béarnaise and the beef sauce from page 176.

MANGO AND COCONUT WITH BRIOCHE PAIN PERDU

Yield – 8 portions

> This is not likely to be created in a home situation due to the specialist equipment and ingredients.
>
> However, we have decided to add it as its creation is interesting.
>
> It resembles a boiled egg and soldiers.

Equipment
Isi whipper cartridges
Cream thermo whip
Round silicon mats

Mango reverse

Ingredients for spherification

50g	caster sugar
50ml	water
450g	mango puree
15g	calcium lactate
3g	xanthan gum

Method

In a saucepan, boil the water and sugar and cool down.

Once cold, mix with the mango purée, calcium lactate and xanthan gum.

Bring to the boil.

Pass the mixture through a fine mesh sieve.

Place the mix in round silicon mats measuring 4 cm diameter by 2cm.

Store in the freezer.

Ingredients – Alginate bath

50g	sugar
8g	sodium alginate
1l	water

Method

In a pan, place the water over a low heat.

Mix the sugar and sodium alginate well and add the mix to the water.

Stir with a high heat spatula until dissolved at 75c.

Pass through a conical sieve over a tall container and allow to cool.

Making the bubbles

Method

Take the silicon mat out of the freezer and pop the frozen domes out of their moulds.

Submerge them in the alginate bath and leave them there for 10 minutes.

They must not touch each other.

With a slotted spoon, move a little in the bath or they will stick to the bottom.

After 10 minutes, remove the bubbles with a slotted spoon and place them in a bowl of warm water in order to remove any excess alginate mixture.

Stock the bubbles in a container full of water in the fridge.

Ingredients – coconut foam

400g	coconut milk, reduced by half to 200g
90g	milk
90g	double cream
20g	Malibu
15g	icing sugar
2 isi	whipper cartridges
1	cream thermo whip

Method

Once the reduced coconut milk has cooled off add all the other ingredients and stir well.

Using a funnel, pour 430g of this mixture into the cream whipper. Close the lid.

Making sure the joint is in place, load 2 cartridges and place the cream whipper in the fridge 15 minutes before use.

Eggy brioche

Ingredients – egg mix

150ml	milk
50g	caster sugar
4	whole egg

Method

Using a hand blender, mix all the ingredients together. Transfer to a shallow tray and keep in the fridge until needed.

Ingredients – brioche soldier

1	slice of brioche

Method

Slice 3x2cm of brioche and dip them in the eggy bread mix, turning over from time to time. You can put them in the night before, but no less than 15 minutes. Cook them in a non-stick frying pan with half olive oil and half fresh butter until firm and golden brown.

When ready, transfer to a chopping board and with a serrated knife trim the outside crust and divide them neatly and equally. Dust some icing sugar on and keep warm

To assemble

Lay 9 porcelain dishes with an 8cm diameter and 3cm depth. Shake the whipper vigorously.

Release the foam neatly in the dishes and with a slotted spoon gently remove the mango bubbles.

Drain carefully and place on top of the foam. Place a brioche soldier next to it and serve immediately.

CHECKERS
pre-dessert

COCONUT GRANITES WITH LIME FOAM
Yield – 4 or 5 servings

> We use this as a refreshing course mid meal, however the granite would make a great dinner party dessert served in tall martini glasses, with diced exotic fruit such as mango & pineapple.
>
> It is possible to do just the granite here and not have the foam.

Equipment
Dehydrator
Hand blender
Thermo whip syphon and 2 cartridges

Ingredients – granite

350g	water
100g	sugar
400g	passed coconut puree
50g	Malibu

Method

In a pan, bring the water and sugar to the boil and leave it to cool.

When cold, pour it over the coconut puree and add the Malibu.

Place in the freezer. Also place your chosen China dishes in the freezer.

Ingredients – lime powder

3   limes

Method

Peel 3 limes and trim the pith. Dry the lime skin in the dehydrator for 8 hours at 68c.

When very dry, blitz through the Braun 750w robo coupe and pass through a pastry sieve. Keep dry.

Lime foam

Ingredients for the liqueur

500ml	water
100g	sugar
7.5g	yellow pectin
3	peeled lime skins

Method

In a saucepan bring the water and sugar to the boil and add the pectin.

Combine using the hand blender.

Cook for 2 minutes. Add the lime skins. Infuse for two hours and pass through a conical sieve.

Keep in the fridge

Ingredients to load the syphon

325g	lime liqueur
100g	passed lime juice
25g	Malibu
60g	egg white

Method

Fill up a thermo whip syphon with the ingredients and load 2 cartridges.

Keep in the fridge.

To assemble

With a fork, scrape the coconut granite until light and airy and generously fill the China dishes previously placed in the freezer.

Shake vigorously the thermo whip syphon and do a little tester on a side plate – it should be glossy and airy.

Spray the coconut elegantly and sprinkle a pinch of lime powder on top.

Serve immediately.

CHECKERS
dessert

SOUFFLÉ NOUGAT

Yield – 4 large china moulds (9.5cm x 6cm)

> At the Checkers, we serve all different kinds of soufflés: fruity, alcoholic, cheesy, with rice pudding, chocolate….the list goes on.
>
> This one is a little more unusual than most.
>
> If serving with a sorbet, we would recommend apricot or raspberry.
>
> It should be something quite sharp to balance the sweetness of the soufflé.

Ingredients – honey crème patissiere

150ml	milk	125g	clear honey
100g	honey	30g	flour
80g	egg yolks		

Method

In a medium size saucepan, bring the milk and 100g of clear honey to the boil and set aside. Whisk the yolks, 125g of honey and the flour and whisk until pale and homogenous.

Pour the milk mix on the egg mix and stir well. Transfer back to the pan. Bring to the boil and cook for 1 minute, whisking continuously. Pass through a fine mesh sieve and keep in a plastic container in the fridge with a lid on.

Roasting the nuts for the outer rim and inside the soufflé mix

50g	whole blanched almonds roasted at 180c 4.30 minutes
35g	whole hazelnuts roasted at 180c for 4.30 minutes
30g	whole pistachios roasted at 180c for 3 minutes

Ingredients – to prepare the moulds

25g	roasted whole blanched almonds, cut in half
25g	roasted whole hazelnuts, cut in half
25g	roasted whole pistachios, cut in half
	soft butter and a pastry brush
	caster sugar

Method

Brush the chilled moulds thoroughly with soft butter and place in the fridge. Wait 10 minutes before applying one more coat but this time stick the roasted nuts all around the mould's rim going half way down. When the nuts are firmly stuck pour some caster sugar in the moulds and in a spinning motion, turn it to cover every inch of the inside of the mould. Keep in the fridge.

Ingredients – mixed nuts for the soufflé mix

Roughly chop the nuts leftover after deducting the ones for the rim.

Ingredients – soufflé mix

120g	egg white
75g	clear honey
150g	honey crème patissiere
10g	Grand Marnier liqueur
10g	chouchen (honey alcohol originally from Brittany)
40g	of the mixed nuts
15g	mixed peel

Method

Heat the honey in a pan and start to whisk the egg white at full speed in a Kenwood Major.

Pour the warm honey into the eggs and beat until a soft peak is reached.

In a saucepan, heat the crème patisiere and once boiling take off the heat. Add the Grand Marnier and the Chouchen and mix well.

Add the mixed nuts and mixed peel.

Add 1/3 of the meringue to the nutty pastry cream mix and whisk thoroughly.

Once done, tip the nutty crème patisiere mix in with the meringue.

Fold gently with a spatula. Divide the mix in the prepared moulds and with a cranked palette knife, smoother the edges and create a dome like shape, clean the side.

Place the soufflés on a tray and bake in a pre-heated oven at 185c for 6-7 minutes, turning the tray and reducing to 180c after 3 minutes.

When well risen and sponge-like to the touch, they are ready.

Dust with icing sugar on the top and serve immediately.

CHECKERS
dessert

DOUBLE CARAMEL CRÈME BRÛLÉE WITH VANILLA PARFAIT

Yield – 6 portions

> These delightful puddings take very little effort but are real crowd-pleasers.
>
> There's something deliciously satisfying about the crack of the caramel as you break into the finished dish with a spoon.
>
> The vanilla parfait is the perfect accompaniment.

Equipment

Kenwood Major bowl (or similar)
Large stainless steel bowl
Maryse
Combi oven
Hand held blender
Blow torch

Ingredients – the vanilla parfait

2	vanilla pods
4	egg yolks
110g	sugar
275g	double cream

Method

With a sharp, serrated knife, split the vanilla pods in two and scrape out the seeds with the back of the knife. Add to the cream. In a Kenwood Major bowl, whisk the cream until you get a ribbon-like consistency. Transfer to a large stainless steel bowl and store in the fridge.

Put the egg yolks into the Kenwood Major with the whisk attachment connected. Place the sugar, moistened with a little water, in a saucepan and bring to 121c. When it reaches that temperature leave it to stand for a minute. Now whisk the egg yolks and pour the syrup onto them. Whisking until tepid. With a maryse, fold the egg-syrup mixture into the vanilla cream until homogenous. Store in an air-tight container in the freezer.

To serve

Take your parfait out of the freezer 5 minutes before starting your crème brûlée. Take the crème brûlée out of the fridge and sprinkle with a good covering of brown sugar. With a hand held blow torch, burn the sugar starting from the outside and working to the centre. When the caramel is still bubbling in the centre, place a nougatine basket in the middle. Put a scoop of parfait in the basket and serve.

Ingredients – caramel crème brûlée mix

1l	double cream
200g	caster sugar
1l	milk
210g	egg yolks

Method

In a large sauce pan, bring cream to the boil. While the cream is boiling, heat the caster sugar gently in a large sauce pan increasing the temperature little by little until it turns a light caramel colour.

Take off the heat and pour the cold milk over it. Bring to the boil. When settled, add the double cream and let it cool in the fridge for 3 hours.

When completely cold, whisk the egg yolk in and pass through a conical sieve. Pour the mix into large dishes and bake in a combi oven at 98c, with a dry heat, for 35-45 minutes. A light wobble is the most accurate of all methods to know when it's cooked. Leave to cool at room temperature then refrigerate.

NOUGATINE BASKET

Ingredients

125g	sugar
65g	glucose
50g	flaked almonds

Method

In a large saucepan, bring the sugar and glucose to a light coloured caramel and add the flaked almonds. Mix well. Transfer the sticky mix onto a pastry tray, lined with a Silpat mat and leave to cool. Using a kitchen hammer, break the nougatine into small chunks. With a hand held blender, blitz the chunks into a fine powder.

Spread the nougatine powder on a pastry tray lined with a Silpat mat into disks around a 10cm diameter. Bake at 180c until golden brown. It should take 5 minutes.

Remove from the oven and let them stand for 45 seconds, then push the disk onto an upside down dariole mould to create the basket. When cold, store in airtight container in a dark, cool place, not a fridge.

CHECKERS
dessert

JÉRÔME TIRAMISU
Yield – 8 portions

> This really good-looking dish is fairly straightforward to make.
>
> There are lots of components that can be made the day before.
>
> This makes a large cake or 8 individual servings.
>
> We temper the chocolate to add that extra final garnish but it would be fine without this.

Equipment
Major Kenwood mixer (or similar)
2x Rhodoid, size 2 (these are clear plastic sheets)

Ingredients – genoise café

4	eggs
125g	sugar
125g	flour
50g	melted butter
7.5g	instant coffee granules dissolved in a little water

Method

In the mixing bowl whisk the egg and sugar lightly at full speed, heating up the outside with a blow torch until the egg mix reaches 50c.

It will increase dramatically in size when stable.

Fold in the flour, then the butter mixed with the coffee.

Lay the mix evenly on a baking tray previously laid with a Silpat mat (or good quality non stick paper) at 180c for 9 minutes.

Turn the tray halfway through cooking to cook the biscuit evenly.

When cooked, turn over on a wire rack and sprinkle some icing sugar on.

Ingredients – coffee punch

150g	water
250g	sugar

Method

Bring to the boil and reserve.

Ingredients – punch

200ml	water
30g	coffee
150g	syrup (ingredients above)

Method

Mix the coffee and the water together. Mix with the syrup. Keep in a plastic container in the fridge.

Ingredients – tiramisu mix

We use rectangular 7x3cm moulds but you can use any shape you like.

100g	amaretto Disarrono
100g	marsala
12g	gelatine, soaked in cold water
4	eggs
325g	sugar
250g	mascarpone
600ml	double cream
2	vanilla pods split in the middle lengthways and scraped with the back of a knife

CHECKERS
dessert

JÉRÔME TIRAMISU   continued

TIRAMISU MIX

Method

Heat up 30g of amaretto and dip the gelatine inside. Dissolve it and pass through a fine mesh sieve. Mix with the remaining amaretto and the Marsala.

To make the pate a bombe – the French term to describe the base mixture for chocolate mousse and similar desserts – dissolve the sugar in a saucepan at a low heat in a bit of water. When completely disolved turn the heat up and bring the syrup to 121c. Meanwhile, in a mixing bowl, whisk the eggs. When the syrup reaches the desired temperature, remove from the heat and drizzle onto the eggs. Beat until tepid.

Turn the speed down and add the gelatine/ amaretto/marsala mix. When completely homogenous, transfer to a big stainless steel bowl.

Keep aside.

In another bowl, whisk the mascarpone, double cream and vanilla seeds until you get a Greek yoghurt consistency. Gently fold the pate a bombe/ marsala mix and the Mascarpone/double cream until homogenous. Fill the moulds and refrigerate.

Ingredients – tempered dark chocolate

Temper your chocolate to make the chocolate slate that sits on top shiny and croquante (snappy).

300g   chopped up or pistole Valrhona Manjari 64%, divided in two different bowls, one with 225g and the other with 75g

Method

In a microwave set on defrost, melt the 300g of dark chocolate in the glass bowl and stir from time to time with a high heat spatula.

The chocolate must achieve 55c.

When the temperature is reached, pour 75g of melted white chocolate in a warm stainless steel bowl and keep it on top of the oven or in a warm pace.

Now add the remaining unmelted chopped up chocolate, that was set aside earlier in the glass bowl.

Stir well with the spatula until the temperature goes down to 28-29c.

When the temperature is reached, add the melted chocolate that was left on top of the oven.

The temperature should reach 31-32c.

If a little under, put back in the microwave for a few seconds.

When 31-32c is reached, the chocolate is tempered.

Finely trap the chocolate between 2 rhodoid, size A2.

Leave to set in the fridge.

Make as many sheets as there is chocolate, as there might be some breakage.

Use one of the moulds you have to set the tiramisu mix, which will give you a guideline on what size to cut the tempered chocolate.

Cut the tempered chocolate neatly with a hot knife.

Keep on a flat plastic tray with a tight lid on at 8c.

We keep all our chocolate in the cellar, where it is nice and cool.

Reserve until needed.

Ingredients – chocolate chantilly

130g	chocolat Manjari Valrhona 64%
140g	cream in a stainless steel bowl
80g	cream in a pan

Method

Melt the chocolate on the defrost setting of the microwave, mixing from time to time.

Whisk the cream in the bowl until you get a light ribbon and keep in the fridge.

Boil the other double cream and add to the melted chocolate. The temperature should be between 45-50c.

Gently fold the chocolate mix with whipped cream until just homogenous and store in a piping bag set with a small plain nozzle.

Keep in the fridge.

Ingredients – amaretto jelly

Prep some square moulds lined tightly with cling film and place them on a flat tray or plate.

200g	water
100g	sugar
2.5g	agar agar powder
105g	amaretto

Method

Boil the water and sugar together and leave to cool. When cold add the agar agar and bring to just below the boil.

Take off the heat and add the amaretto. Mix well and pour into the cling film lined moulds. Set in the fridge.

Ingredients – coffee ice cream

275g	double cream
115g	caster sugar
4	yolks
8g	instant coffee granules dissolved in a little water

Method

In a stainless steel bowl, whisk the cream until you get a Greek yoghurt consistency and keep in the fridge. To make the pate a bombe, dissolve the sugar in a saucepan at a low heat in a little water.

When completely dissolved, turn the heat up and bring the syrup to 121c. Meanwhile, in a Kenwood Major mixing bowl, whisk the eggs yolks. When the syrup reaches the temperature, remove from the heat and pour onto the eggs.

Beat until cool. Add the coffee. Fold with the cream, which was previously whisked. Taste and add more coffee if you prefer it stronger.

Freeze.

Ingredients – toasted almonds

100g	whole flaked almonds
35g	icing sugar
10cl	kirsch

Method

Colour the almonds on a roasting tray for 4 minutes at 160c. Take them out, sprinkle the icing sugar and the kirsch evenly and return to the oven for another 2-3 minutes. Leave to cool on the tray and keep dry. Store in an air tight container.

To assemble and serve

15 minutes before you serve, put the tray of amaretto cream in the freezer.
Cut the coffee genoise to the same size as the amaretto cream and dab it generously with coffee punch. Take the amaretto cream out of the freezer and remove from the moulds using a blow torch to loosen the edges if needed.

Put directly onto the pre-cut genoise. Pipe some regular dots of chocolate Chantilly on the top. Lift the tiramisu base onto the cold plate and scatter a few toasted almonds on the other side. Put a scoop of coffee ice cream on the almonds and place the tempered chocolate tuille on the chocolate Chantilly. Serve immediately.

PASSION FRUIT AND WHITE CHOCOLATE CIGARETTE

Yield – 10 portions

> This dessert is a real crowd pleaser, and that's no surprise.
>
> Even if we say so ourselves it looks stunning.
>
> But more importantly, it's a perfect vehicle for great summery flavours.
>
> It works best with delicious seasonal fruit.
>
> I suppose it takes its cues from one of the great classics – strawberries and cream.
>
> It transforms what might be a simple pairing into an elegant and refined dish.

Ingredients – mousse

180g	passion fruit puree
2	large egg yolks
30g	caster sugar
360g	good quality white chocolate – in small pieces
480g	whipping cream

Method

Whip the whipping cream to very soft peaks and set aside at room temperature.

Quickly whisk together the egg yolks and sugar in a bowl and add the passion fruit puree.

Place the bowl over a bain-marie filled with simmering water and continuously whisk to a minimum of 75c.

Remove from the heat and stir in the chocolate.

Place the bowl back over the bain-marie and stir the mixture until it reaches 43°c.

At this stage all the chocolate will have melted.

Remove from the heat and add all the soft whipped cream at once.

Fold gently and place in a container.

Refrigerate.

NOUGATINE

Ingredients

250g   sugar
125g   glucose
         small amount of water
100g   flaked almonds

Method

Bring water, sugar and glucose to a caramel point.

Add the flaked almonds and incorporate with a heatproof spatula. Cool it on the pastry tray.

When the mixture is completely cool, break it with a hammer first and the mix it with a hand blender until it resembles a powder.

Sprinkle on parchment paper thinly and cook in the oven for approximately 10 minutes at 180c.

Once golden in colour, remove from the oven, cut and roll your cigarette around a cylinder of the desired size and shape. If it hardens while you are doing that, just put it back in the oven for a minute. Let the cylinders cool and keep them in an air tight container until required.

HOW TO SERVE

On a rectangular plate, dress the fruit salad in an attractive manner.

Put a few dots of coulis on the fruit salad and some passion fruit seeds.

Using a piping bag, fill the cigarette with passion fruit and white chocolate mousse at the very last minute and serve at once.

PASSION FRUIT AND WHITE CHOCOLATE CIGARETTE continued

Ingredients – red fruit coulis

200g strawberries
Sugar syrup to taste

Method

Blitz together and pass through a conical sieve, keep in a squeezy bottle.

Ingredients - seasonal fruit salad

100g   strawberries
100g   raspberry
100g   blueberries
100g   blackberries
         a few passion fruit seeds

DOME OF WHITE CHOCOLATE CREMEUX, POACHED RHUBARB, RHUBARB PEARL AND CANDIED GINGER

Yield – 6 portions

This is a beautiful dessert that is aesthetically pleasing and has a flavour that is second to none.

We have tried a lot of different chocolate brands over the years but Valrhona, in our opinion, is vastly superior to any other.

A bit of practice might be required to get the tempering right but it is definitely worth the effort.

Equipment

3 sets of 6 chocolate sphere moulds (7cm diameter and 4cm depth). Ensure scrupulously cleaned and finished with cotton wool
2 glass bowls (they retain the heat better)
1 stainless steel bowl (kept warm)
1 microwave
1 high heat resistant spatula
1digital thermometer
1 Scottish scraper
Tall blender jug
Combi oven

Ingredients – white chocolate sphere

Tempering will make the dome shiny and croquant (snappy).

600g   chopped up or pistole Valrhona Ivoire 35% divided in two different bowls, one with 450g and the other with 150g

Method

In a microwave set on defrost, melt the 450g of white chocolate in the glass bowl and stir from time to time with the high heat spatula.

The chocolate must reach 45-48c. When the temperature is reached, pour 150g of melted white chocolate in a warm stainless steel

bowl and keep it on top of the oven or in a warm pace. Now add the remaining unmelted, chopped-up chocolate that was earlier set aside in the glass bowl.

Stir well with the spatula until the temperature goes down to 26-27c. When the temperature is reached, add the melted chocolate that was left on top of the oven or Aga.

The temperature should be 28-29c. If a little under, put back in the microwave for a few seconds.

When 28-29c is reached, the chocolate is tempered. Pour it over the sphere moulds.

Make sure the tempered chocolate has reached every part of the moulds. Be quick and precise and using a Scottish scraper, tap the moulds gently to remove any excess of chocolate.

Tip it over to drain over a tray.

Repeat the operation with the remaining 2 moulds. Keep the moulds in the fridge.

Take the domes out of the moulds by laying a clean cloth on the table and tapping the mould lightly on it.

Keep the sphere in an air-tight box in the fridge.

201

DOME OF WHITE CHOCOLATE CREMEUX, POACHED RHUBARB, RHUBARB PEARL AND CANDIED GINGER continued

Ingredients – ivoire cremeux

225g   pistols white Ivoire chocolate
6g   bronze gelatin soaked in a bit of water
5   egg yolks
50g   caster sugar
250ml   whole milk
250ml   double cream
50g   cognac

Method

Melt the chocolate in a glass bowl in a microwave set on defrost. In a stainless steel bowl, whisk the egg yolks and sugar until thick and pale. Add the double cream and milk to the bowl and transfer to a saucepan.

Heat to 29c, stirring all the time. When the temperature is reached, transfer to a large stainless steel bowl. Heat up 10cl of cognac and dissolve the gelatine in it then add to the custard, quickly followed by the remaining cognac.

Emulsify with a hand blender for 2 minutes until smooth and creamy.

Slowly pour 1/3 of the custard onto the melted white chocolate and using a spatula draw small and quick circles in the centre. Repeat the techniques with the second and third amounts.

Emulsify again with the hand blender for 1 more minute. Transfer to a stainless steel bowl and cover with cling film to prevent a skin from forming. Rest for 12 hours.

The following day, fill the spheres with the cremeux.

Ingredients – poached rhubarb

800g   washed and peeled Champagne rhubarb
         and cut in batons with an angle
700ml   sweet wine, Monbazillac or Sauternes
50ml   grenadine
100g   caster sugar
1   vanilla pod cut in half lengthways
Peel   of 1 orange

Method

Place all the rhubarb batons on a deep baking tray. In a large saucepan bring the sweet wine, the grenadine, sugar, vanilla and orange peel to the boil and pour over on the rhubarb. Cover with baking parchment then foil, making sure there is a tight seal around the dish.

Bake at 160c for 20 minutes, with the full fan on. Check it after 10 minutes. Cool at room temperature.

Ingredients – rhubarb caviar pearl (spherification)

300ml	rhubarb poaching liquor
3g	sodium alginate
20g	caster sugar

Calcium bath

1lt	water
10g	calcium chloride
1	spherical caviar dispenser

Method

In a mixing bowl, whisk the poaching liquor at speed 2. In a small stainless steel bowl, mix the sodium alginate and the sugar thoroughly together and add slowly to the liquor, like when pouring syrup into a meringue. Refrain from touching the whisk as it will stick to it. Whisk for 10 minutes. Leave the mixture to rest for an additional 10 minutes. The mixture should be quite thick and smooth.

For the calcium bath, place the water into a tall and thin measuring jug. Add the calcium chloride and stir with a spatula until dissolved.

Load up the spherical caviar dispenser and hold it above the calcium chloride solution. Stir the water to help shape round balls. Leave in the bath for 3 minutes to allow a skin to form.

Pour the jug over a pastry sieve and rinse with cold water. Keep the caviar pearls in a bit of poaching liquor in an air tight container in the fridge.

Ingredients – rhubarb coulis

150g	poaching liquor
75g	sugar
1	vanilla pod cut in half lenghtways
300g	washed, peeled and roughly chopped Champagne rhubarb
50g	monbazillac or Sauternes
20cl	grenadine
100g	poaching liquor
3g	agar agar

Method

In a large saucepan put the liquor, vanilla and caster sugar and bring to the boil. When boiling add the rhubarb and cook through. You are looking for a puree-like consistency. Take out the vanilla pod and add the white wine and the grenadine.

Transfer the mix to a tall blender jug and blitz for 90 seconds, until very smooth. Pass through a conical sieve. Taste and correct the acidity and colour by adding some grenadine and caster sugar if necessary. In a separate pan, bring the 100ml of poaching liquor and the agar to the boil, whisking all the time. Once boiling, pour it into the rhubarb mix with the machine running. Transfer to a stainless steel tray and leave to set in the fridge for 90 minutes.

Clean the blender jug and once time has elapsed, transfer the set rhubarb puree in it and blend until you get a luscious, fragrant coulis. Taste and correct the sharpness with grenadine and thickness with a bit more of poaching liquor. Pass through a fine mesh sieve and reserve in a squeezy bottle.

Ingredients – Sable Breton

100g	nibbed almonds
100g	caster sugar
100g	flour
100g	ground almonds
100g	diced salted butter at room temperature

Method

In a stainless steel mixing bowl, blend the nibbed almonds, the sugar, the flour and the ground almonds thoroughly. Add the soft butter (beurre pomade) and grind everything together until homogenous but crumbly. Lay the mix evenly on a pastry tray prepared with a Silpat and cook in a Rational oven with a dry heat and full fan at 170c for 7-10 minutes, until golden brown. Pull the Silpat from the baking tray, with the crumble on, and cool on a work surface. When cold, transfer to a small container with a lid and store in a dry and dark place.

Ingredients – pickled ginger
See page 104

To assemble

Using a paint brush and some melted butter, paint a strip on the side of the plate and scatter some sable Breton on and shake off the surplus. Drain some rhubarb batons and place nicely on the side of the plate and scatter a few pieces of candied ginger. With a Parisienne scoop, dig a hole in the middle of the cremeux and and fill it with the rhubarb pearls. Place a slither of candied ginger on top and put the dome over the rhubarb batons. Squirt some coulis tastefully on the side of the plate. Finish with a ½ empty shell and sprig of mint.

SARAH'S MARVELLOUS CHOCOLATE TART WITH STEM GINGER PARFAIT

Yield – 1 large tart or 3 small

This is simple but also very good.

It is great served warm or cold and works brilliantly with a variety of ice creams – mint, vanilla, ginger or coffee.

It is the best chocolate tart I have ever tasted.

Equipment

Kenwood Major mixer

Ingredients – the short bread pastry

This brilliant recipe might yield slightly more than needed, but well-wrapped in cling film it will freeze very well.

300g	soft butter
150g	icing sugar
2g	salt
3	egg yolks
375g	flour
45g	ground almonds

Method

In a mixing bowl, knead the butter, icing sugar and salt with the paddle at speed 1 for 2 minutes.

Add the egg yolks and mix for another minute.

Add the flour and almonds and knead for 30 seconds until the dough has combined.

Wrap in cling film and rest in the fridge for 2 hours.

Prepping the tins

Using a pastry brush and soft butter, coat the inside of a 23 cm diameter fluted tart tin.

Laying the dough

Place the dough between two sheets of lightly floured baking parchment and roll the pastry down using a rolling pin.

Take it down to 0.4cm all over and leave in the fridge to harden for 15 minutes.

The pastry needs to rest to avoid shrinking when it is being cooked.

When done, peel the baking parchment and line the buttered/floured tart moulds, making sure there are no holes.

The top should hang by 2cm.

Blind bake at 150c for 7-10 minutes.

Regularly open the door to egg wash the inside of the tarts, making them impermeable.

When cooked, leave to cool in the moulds.

When cold, trim the outer lip with a small serrated knife.

SARAH'S MARVELLOUS CHOCOLATE TART WITH STEM GINGER PARFAIT continued

Ingredients – chocolate tart mix

300g	Valrhona Caraibe chocolate 64% pistols
115g	butter
150g	double cream
5	whole eggs
2	yolks
115g	caster sugar

Method

Put the chocolate, butter and double cream in a stainless steel bowl and place it over a large pan of water on a medium heat, to melt it. In a separate bowl whisk the eggs, egg yolks and sugar together until pale.

Using a spatula, fold the chocolate and the egg mixture together and fill the lined, cooked pastry case.

Cook in a pre-heated oven at 140c for 20 minutes.

Ingredients – stem ginger parfait

275g	double cream
4	egg yolks
110g	sugar
	to taste, neatly diced stem ginger
	to taste, ginger powder

Method

In a stainless steel bowl, whip the double cream to a Greek yoghurt consistency. Cover with cling film and keep in the fridge. Place the egg yolks in a Kenwood Major mixing bowl with the whisk attachment ready to go. In a saucepan, bring the sugar and a little water to 121c.

When it has reached that temperature, turn off the heat and leave it to stand on the side for a minute. Start to whisk the egg yolks in the mixer and gently but continuously tip the syrup into the yolks.

Beat until completely cold. Using a spatula, fold the double cream and egg mixture together until homogenous. Add the diced stem ginger and the powdered ginger (to taste).

Freeze.

Nougatine basket

See recipe page 191

To assemble

Warm up your dessert plate and take the tarts out of the moulds.

Present on an appropriate dish. Scoop some ginger ice cream into the nougatine basket and serve on the side.

Serve.

Ingredients – pate a foncer or lining pastry

If you find the short bread pastry too daunting, this fool proof recipe is a great substitute. It was originally for quiches and small tartlettes, which needed to stay crisp.

250g	soft butter
20g	caster sugar
12.5g	salt
2	eggs
500g	flour
80g	water

Method

In a mixing bowl, knead the soft butter, sugar and salt and eggs with the paddle at speed 1 for 3 minutes. Add the flour and knead for 30 seconds until the mixture has almost combined together. Add the water and knead for 30 seconds, until just about smooth. Do not over work.

Wrap neatly in cling film and rest in the fridge for at least 2 hours before using.

CHECKERS
chocolates

SELECTION OF HANDMADE VALRHONA CHOCOLATES

"All of the chocolates at The Checkers are tempered in-house, following a set of clear rules set by the best Chocolatiers in France. They all follow the same courbe de temperature.

There are three key stages, the first is the melting then there is crystallisation and finally it's manual work.

First and foremost, the moulds have to be scrupulously clean and brushed with cotton balls then the tempering can begin. The tempering will make the chocolate shiny and croquant (snappy).

Now pour the tempered chocolate in your clean mould and when all areas are covered, tap the mold with a spatula leave to set in the fridge. When set pipe your chosen filling in and when set close the chocolate with tempered chocolate."

White chocolate

Dulcey, Ivoire, Opalys tempers at:
1st (A) temp 45/48c 2nd (B) temp 26/27c 3rd (C) temp 28/29c

Milk chocolate

Jivara Lactee tempers at:
1st (A) temp 45-48c 2nd (B) temp 27-28c 3rd (C) temp 29-30c

Dark chocolate

Tempers at:
1st (A) temp 55-58c 2nd (B) temp 28-29c 3rd (C) temp 31-32c

Ingredients for 2 trays of x 27 chocolates each

300g   chopped chocolate divided in two different bowls, one with 225g and the other with 75g

Method

In a microwave set on defrost, melt the 225g of chocolate in the glass bowl and stir from time to time with the high heat spatula. The chocolate must achieve **TEMPERATURE A**.
When the temperature is reached pour 75g of the melted chocolate into a warm stainless steel bowl and keep warm. Now add the remaining, unmelted 75g of chopped chocolate to the glass bowl. Stir well with the spatula until the temperature goes down to **TEMPERATURE B**.
When the temperature is reached, add the reserved melted chocolate and the temperature should reach **TEMPERATURE C**.
If a little under, put back in the microwave for a few seconds. When temperature c is reached, the chocolate is tempered.

CHECKERS
chocolates

Ingredients – Chocolat noir Manjari 64% chocolate fillings

65g   jivara lactee pistols
250g   praline

Method

Melt the chocolate in a glass bowl in the microwave set on defrost. Mix with a spatula from time to time. Add the praline and whisk thoroughly.

Pass through a pastry tamis and place in a disposable piping bag. Fill the tempered chocolate neatly.

Put the whole chocolate tray in the fridge for 20 minutes and close them with tempered chocolate.

Ingredients – Chocolat au lait jivara 40% interieur caramel beurre sale

200g   sugar
25g   water
100ml double cream
100g   salted butter
2g   salt de Guerande

Method

In a large saucepan, make a dark caramel with the sugar and the water and stop the cooking process with the cream, which might spit.

Then add the butter and salt. Whisk well and cool. When cold enough to handle, transfer to a disposable piping bag. The filling cannot be hotter than 27c.

Fill the chocolate cavity in the moulds and place in the fridge for 30 minutes. Close the chocolate with the remaining tempered chocolate.

Ingredients – chocolat blanc Ivoire

150g   dessicated coconut
70g   coconut milk
200g   Malibu
16g   sugar
175g   Ivoire blanc chocolate

Method

Lightly toast the coconut in the oven at 150c for 8-10 minutes.

Meanwhile melt the chocolate in a glass bowl in a microwave set on defrost, mixing from time to time. In a saucepan, mix the coconut milk and the Malibu at 50c.

Make a caramel with the sugar and when golden brown, deglaze with the coconut milk and the Malibu.

Pour the caramel on to the chocolate using the kernel method, 1/3 at a time, really working the caramel into the chocolate.

Then add the toasted coconut. When below 27c, fill up the tempered chocolate moulds and leave in the fridge for 24 hours.

The next day, close the chocolate with tempered Ivoire white chocolate.

Ingredients Chocolat Dulce 34%

175g   Chocolat blanc Ivoire Valrhona
100g   double cream
75g   Baileys (it also works with Tia Maria)

Method

In a glass bowl melt the chocolate in the microwave set on defrost, mixing from time to time with a spatula.

Add the warm cream to the chocolate 1/3 at a time mixing well, using the kernel technique.

Add the Baileys and emulsify with the hand blender.

When cool enough to handle, transfer to a disposable piping bag and fill up the lined chocolate moulds with the mix, leaving enough space to close.

Keep in the fridge for 24 hours. The next day, close with tempered Dulce chocolate.

CHECKERS
producer

THE ART OF FOOD

By Dominic Robertson

"The presentation of the food at the Checkers is an art in itself. It is an in-built part of the experience. It's a fantastic visual feast before you even get to taste it."

You can forgive artists for talking in artistic terms but Susan Robertson's description of Stephane Borie's food is one that comes from experience.

The Mid Wales artist has dined at the Checkers on a number of occasions – it is a dead heat between the boudon noir and the scallops for her favourite dish, with the puddings a close second.

But unlike the rest of the restaurant's patrons, she has also used her skills to capture Mr Borie's food in her own beautifully simplistic and stylised drawings. For diners visiting the restaurant, if they can look away from the treat on their plate and glance along the walls, they will find Susan's two dimensional representations of the chef's signature dishes, capturing the visual splendour of Michelin Star dining.

Susan, from the tranquil nearby Mid Wales village of Kerry, has used the talents initially nurtured by her art-teacher parents, developed at West Surrey College of Art and Design, and then refined through a lifetime of drawing for pleasure, to produce a series of pictures depicting the colours and the shapes that wow so many diners and critics alike.

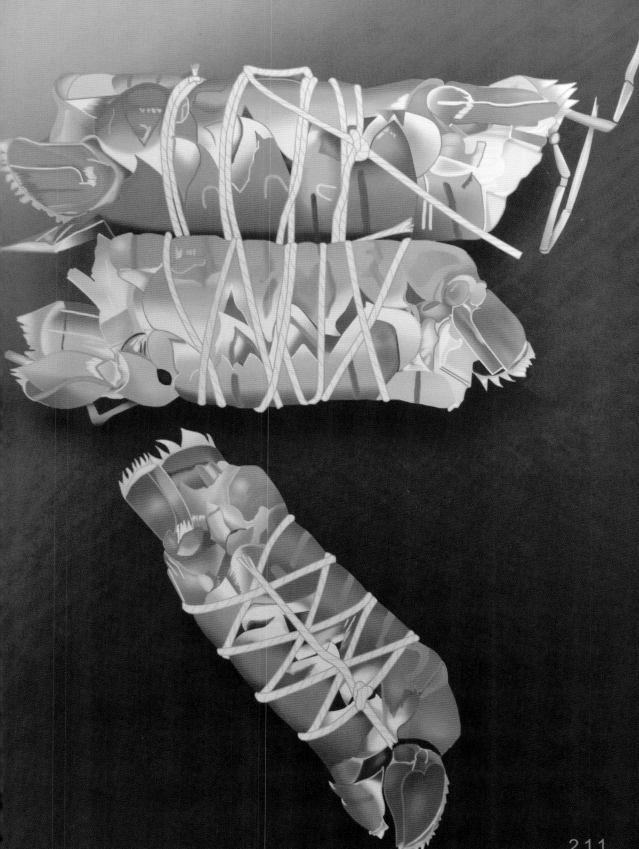

211

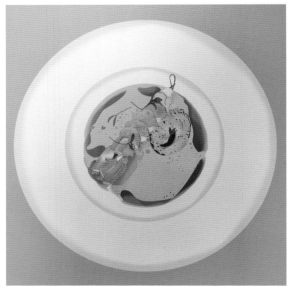

The role-call includes the courgette fleur stuffed with Cornish crab, a Scottish scallop tomato and langoustine, baked scallops, caramelised apple and calvados ravioli in cider sauce, and king langoustines, baby gem and squid ink ravioli.

Last but not least an assiette du pecher consisting of langoustine tail, poached Dover sole, black truffle sandwich and nantua sauce.

The artwork might never have happened but for a rainy day, which meant fewer customers in the gallery where Susan worked, opposite the Checkers.

"It was a very wet day and quiet in the gallery and I just decided to draw the Checkers opposite," she said.

"Not long after I had finished it, I attended one of Stephane's canapé courses and at the end I thought "shall I give it to him?".

I did and he was really pleased which was fantastic because it's always funny giving someone your artwork – they might hate it and just be polite!"

Stephane was so enamoured with the piece that it has since appeared in a number of guises at the restaurant, leading the chef to ask her if she would bend her talents to a special commission – a drawing of a series of puddings created by Stephane's wife Sarah to be given as her Christmas gift.

With that commission successfully navigated Susan took some persuading to graduate to the savoury courses but found herself captivated by the shapes and patterns once she started.

She said: "I had never drawn food before at all and Stephane asked me if I would like to draw some of his dishes.

"I initially said no because it was not something I had done, but having thought about it I looked at a couple of the dishes and I could see how they might take shape and thought it might be quite exciting and different to try it.

"You can't just say Stephane is a cook or a chef, the construction of the dishes is a sight to behold, they truly are works of art.

"You look at the way the sauces make beautiful patterns and the way the dishes are constructed, the way they are put together."

The process of creation takes slightly longer than the edible version, with around five days of work going into each piece of art.

It's a process that begins in pencil, with the shape of the dish and develops from there.

Once happy with the image it is scanned into a computer and coloured using what amounts to a digital pen. Susan said that the key is always about representing what you actually see.

"Whatever I draw I look for shapes and patterns in it," she said. So for example, if it's a building it is either the brickwork or the windows and how they work together to create the shapes.

"My father always says you have to really look at things and put down what you see and not what you think you see."

LOCAL PRODUCE IS KEY INGREDIENT

It's important to us to build strong relationships with local producers. They're the lifeblood of the farming community that surrounds Montgomery.

One great example is Neuadd Fach Baconry, which is just up the road from us in the quiet village of Llandinam.

It is home to Lynda and Ithyl Brown and has established itself as a well-known producer of pork products. We've had a great supply from them for many years and they've won more than 30 Great Taste awards, which is no mean feat.

Lynda and Ithyl have diversified over the years to make a go of their business. They once supported a dairy herd and in 1982 sheep were added.

However, the couple recognised the need to diversify and in 1986 a brand new building was put up to 'loose house' the new herd of pigs.

Ithyl, who hails from Caersws, bought the smallholding in 1963 and Lynda, who was brought up in Uxbridge in Middlesex, came to live at Neuadd Fach with her sons David and Philip, when she married Ithyl in 1979.

"Farming isn't easy," says Lynda. "It's important to have good partnerships with restaurants like The Checkers.

"They can trust us to supply them with the best quality products and we have a good relationship with them, where we can forecast what they might need in a given period."

For us, it's great to have people like Lynda and Ithyl just down the road.

They've endured difficult times but pulled through with dogged determination and an uncompromising attitude.

They opened their baconry in 1999 and it's grown considerably, going from strength to strength.

The couple have won Gold Awards for their products in the Great Taste Awards over the years.

Lynda adds: "We aim to provide the best tasting products by attention to detail. Our pigs are fed a ration that is mixed on the farm ensuring a superb carcass to start with.

"Our carcasses are hung for 5 days before they are processed and we measure the cure for our bacon and gammon very accurately to ensure a consistent product.

"Our curing takes 10 days, and then we slice and package very carefully to ensure the product looks good.

"The proof of our care is in the eating.

"The taste is paramount to us, and many people say that once you taste our bacon you don't want anyone else's. We weren't butchers to start with but we learned our way and as they say the proof is in the pudding now."

Working with people like Lynda and Ithyl means we get precisely what we need.

The taste of their product is second to none and we have numerous partnerships with great producers like them. It's all about putting brilliant produce onto the plate. People like Lynda and Ithyl make that possible.

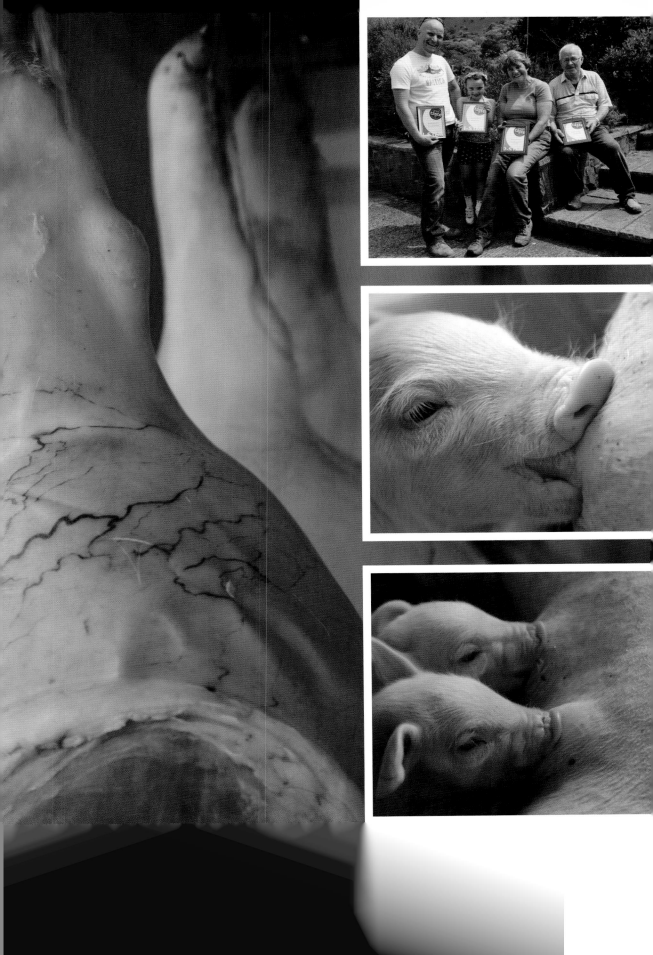

THE CHECKERS EXPERIENCE

By Kathryn Francis

In our earliest days, at The Herbert Arms, in Chirbury, we were bringing something new to the local restaurant scene.

We knew that the right welcome would dispel the myths of grandeur from the 'French Chef' and the locals would give us a chance.

Our fledgling customer base soon realised that Stéphane's skills in the kitchen and the relaxed but professional hospitality meant that they could enjoy a delicious dining experience.

As local farmers daughters we understood our location and that the right level of 'hospitality' was key – and this approach is something that we have carried forward to The Checkers.

We want their dinner or overnight stay to be relaxing and comfortable. It ought to be about them – not us.

When guests join us we try not to interfere.

You won't find our team hovering around tables, we don't want to interrupt conversations or court compliments.

We hope to anticipate what guests need, and be there when they need us. We love to have a good chat with customers – if they want to – but otherwise we like to let guests get on and enjoy themselves.

CHECKERS
rooms and hinterland

CHECKERS
rooms and hinterland

Key to this is an experienced front of house staff team. Sarah or I always lead service and Leanne is our number two, a local girl and a real asset to our team – she is the very best in home grown talent.

There is nothing better than a smooth service and a dining room buzzing with chatter and laughter. Our mission is quite simple: we want guests to enjoy one another's company while being served great food by a pleasant, professional team. It's like being the host at a really good party – and we love it.

Communication with the kitchen is key – and Stéphane is always keen for feedback that all is well front of house, especially if we have a new dish on the menu. He spends hours thinking about a dish, executing it and then refining it… but ultimately it is what our customers think that counts.

Today we have guests from our local area, and there's quite a strong following.
As the business has evolved, they have started to use us differently.

We used to have guests who would come once a fortnight to the Herbert Arms. Now people come less often – a special occasion destination for birthdays and anniversaries.
There are plenty of people who travel from further afield, particularly those who use the rooms.

CHECKERS
rooms and hinterland

When we renovated The Checkers and designed our rooms, it was important that everything was suited to the area. We didn't want to be country twee. We wanted to be stylish while also being comfortable and homely.

The rooms took a long time to develop – as a Grade Two Listed building in a conservation area it was not a straightforward project and we had a budget!

We spent months and months liaising with the guy who was drawing up the plans, as well as with the planners and conservation officer.

At one stage, the conservation officer wanted us to put the bedrooms on one side of the building and the bathrooms on the other. But common sense won, with some compromises on both parts.

Sarah and I prioritised the things we love in nice hotels for the rooms – comfortable beds, good linen & towels, toiletries that are lovely to use and of course homemade cookies, high quality loose leaf tea and coffee and plenty of fresh milk.

When guests stay with us it is a bit of a treat – we want the little touches to make that treat a bit more special.

Maintaining standards and attention to detail is as important in the rooms as it is in the kitchen – fundamental to this is our housekeeping team. Kate Richardson has been with us since our early days at The Herbert Arms and for Kate there is never 'good enough' – she has delivered 100% and cared about The Checkers as much as we do – this is a special thing to find.

We feel very lucky to be a part of Montgomery, as for us, it is the most beautiful gateway to Wales. I remember the first time I went to the town – it felt like an oasis.

It's an undiscovered gem somehow combining quaint charm, sophistication and a real sense of belonging.

This, together with the marches borderland is quite special – the Peak District and Lake District might have great reputations, but they are no more beautiful and the footfall is so high – a walk around Montgomery can be solitary in the very best way.

Sarah and I grew up on our parent's dairy farm, New Barns, in Shropshire, about 20 miles from Montgomery. We really are products of our upbringing.

Now we see our children being shaped by our work and where they live. Of course there are compromises, but for us Montgomery is a special place to spend your childhood and they are seeing first hand that you reap what you sow – and that can only serve them well on their own adventures.

I hope they will feel the same pride for The Checkers that we feel for New Barns.

Our business has thrived because although we all bring a different skill to the table we are united by the same ethos, vision and goal – hard work, happy guests and a healthy business.

We love our countryside restaurant with rooms and thankfully so do many of our guests. Long may that continue.

CHECKERS
thank yous

CHECKERS
thank yous

The Checkers and this book is a team effort and these are our thank yous – some professional, some personal.

Michel Roux Snr, for writing the foreword and being
the ultimate culinary inspiration.

Andy Richardson, at A Way With Media – professional, dedicated
and uncompromising in the best possible way.

Paul Naylor, our designer, who works until 4am on last minute changes
and has understood what we have wanted to achieve. Thank you.

Special thanks go to key members of our team:

Jerome epitomises hard work, passion and dedication. A farmer's son from Brittany, he is a true
Checkers boy who brings grit, skill and a hunger to succeed. You will go far.

Kate has been with us since our early days at The Herbert Arms and no one understands these
farmer's daughters better! We will always be grateful Mrs R. You have been there when we needed you most.

Leanne is unassuming, competent beyond her years and lovely to work with.
She is our cappuccino queen who copes in a crisis and we love her a lot!

Our Mum and Dad, Helen and Roger, for believing in us, teaching us what hard work can achieve
and that juggling all the balls can be difficult but not impossible.

Profound thank you to the Dupont Family, Jacqueline, Serge, Mamie Elizabeth and godfather Rene for their
invaluable guidance during my early years and total faith in my abilities! Merci de tout Coeur.

Our kids – Lexie, Roxie, Emme, Fabien and Joseph – you are a cracking bunch who cope with your
sometimes busy, tired and distracted parents brilliantly. We love you all more than you can know.

Finally, Kathryn's biggest thank you is to Neil, her partner, for his unending support,
faith and pride. Life with a Francis girl is never easy!

The Frenchman & the Farmer's Daughters